Traveling
Toward
Transformation

—By *Travena Rogan*—

Sis Debbie, TODAY +
GoD BLESS you such a
Always FOR being + Godly
wonderful heart d soul—
blessing to my your hand in
I shall follow heaven!! through
hand toward refreshment through
You are my beautiful Father)—
Him (our Love Always

Dedication

This book is dedicated to two special men in my life, Will and Darrien Rogan.

To my wonderful husband Will, God's most rare gift to accompany me on this side of life. Every day you help me travel toward transformation, as your wife and the mother of our son. I would want no one else to walk this journey with. Thanks for your patience in allowing me to complete my dream of Christian authorship. Thanks for the nights you allowed me to disturb your sleep to listen to another chapter idea. Thanks for always being in my corner, loving me unconditionally, and expecting nothing in return, but for me to love God and you.

Darrien – God created such a sweet and kind-spirited boy for me to love and teach about our heavenly Father. May you always know, and appreciate God's love. As you grow, mature, and prayerfully someday choose to follow God, may your feet be firmly planted toward following God, studying His Word, and living by His principles. Thank you for allowing me to interrupt your play time as I wrote this book. I would trade places with none other. I love being your Mom!

In Memory of

Doris Ann Gregory-Walker (my Mom) – God so blessed me with a mom that practiced what she preached. She was not afraid to say she was wrong or apologize if needed. She was my first teacher of how to be a lady and to love God. My heart swells with joy every time I think of her and reflect upon her words of wisdom.

Calvin Keith Walker (my Big Brother) – Not many girls will get ther privilege or perk of having a true big brother! H was my protector, my support, my laughter, my joy. The stamina he exhibited reminds me daily to keep going!

Sister Helen Scott (my Christian Mom – "Two are better than one..." (Ecc. 3:5). What a godly lady, influence, and friend! Her words of wisdom still echo in my heart and give me the opportunity to share her wisdom with others. My life will never be the same for having known her.

Sister Dorothy Woods – One of my biggest fans, she is one of the reasons I wrote this book. Her desire to know God's Word and express the desire to have someone study with her leaves me with so many fond memories of sweet days gone by.

Brother Barry – I thank God for allowing me to know him for a little while. His desire and forwardness to see this manuscript come to life was so touching. He would be pleased.

I would also like to thank—

To my heavenly Father for continually molding me into what He desires for me to be. I thank You for this privilege of writing the words

You put on my heart. May You be glorified in all that I say and do. Thank You for answering my prayers and giving me such a fulfilling and humbling opportunity.

Dorita Lowe – My beautiful sister, thanks for listening, believing, and encouraging me, not just for this endeavor, but for all I've ever done. You are truly a meek and godly sister. I love you!

Daddy (Daddio) – Thanks for never being surprised by anything I set out to do. You have always believed that I could accomplish anything that I would set my mind to do. I love you!

Brian Scott – I love the artistic ability that God has blessed you with. Thanks for the creation of my cover art and making my words visionary. You are a sweet and humble spirit.

Tammy Belcher – May Baby and former "Priscilla Class" student. God bless you for contributing your poem. You're a great poet and truly a girl after God's own heart! I am blessed to know you and call you my friend.

Brother Homer Malone – Thanks for being just as excited about my book as I was. Thanks for always listening and giving me godly, wise advice throughout my Christian journey. I can always call upon you, and you are there.

Brother Dewayne Scott – My big brother! Thanks for your advice, business knowledge, excitement, encouragement, and prayers. You are a man of many talents, and I am blessed to have you in my corner.

Brother Terry Reynolds – My fellow laborer in the gospel. You are as sound as Paul and firmly planted in the truth, like a tree planted by the rivers of water. God is continually doing great things with you.

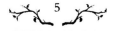

It has been a privilege and a blessing to have your support on this journey. God bless you always to be steadfast.

Sister Betty Barkley – My breath of fresh air! You are what I hope to become when I grow up. I am blessed to have you as a frend and fellow laborer in the gospel. I thank God upon every rememberance of you. Thanks for your sacrificial support.

My Dear Friends (Elaine, Christi, Regina, and Miriam) – The Lord has blessed me with a special select few that rejoice when I rejoice and weep when I weep. I will forever be indebted to each of you for your unconditional support and genuine love.

The staff of 21st Century Christian – Thank you, thank you for all that each of you have done to help my book come to life. God bless you always for glorifying Him!

Renee – Thanks for your help and unending dedication. You are a true Christian striving to please the Master. Thanks for seeing me and not the color of my skin. I will always be grateful for your support and drive to see my book in print

Contents

Preface..9

Section One: Honesty With Self Is the Best Policy

1. A Look on the Inside..13
2. Forgetting Those Things 25
3. Come Out With Your Hands Up 31

Section Two: The Jackhammer

4. Counting the Cost 39
5. Cannot See for Looking 47
6. I Must Be About My Father's Business 55
7. I Must Develop a Thankful Heart 65

Section Three: The Eye Opener

8. Survival of the Faithful 77
9. We Are Just Passing Through.............................89
10. Awake Thou That Sleepest 93

Section Four: The Cleanser

11. The Goodness of God 101
12. Getting to Know All About God 111
13. The Peacefulness of Surrendering.................121

Preface

This book has been written for all those searching for peace in the wrong places. Does anger have you acting out? Is past pain holding you hostage? Is depression your best friend? Has an unhappy marriage derailed you? Do your children have you ready to run? Has "new mommy" syndrome gotten the best of you? Is your spiritual woman being hindered by the troubles of life? Do you get upset over the smallest things? Do you find pleasure in keeping bad company? Does your life seem to be spinning out of control? Are you in a place you thought you would never be? Do you feel far away from God? If you answered "yes" to any or all of these questions, keep reading.

Knowing God isn't something you do occasionally. It's a conscious, deliberate effort to develop a daily relationship with God. To know God requires desire, discipline, and determination. Therefore, you become released from the bondage of guilt, frustration, and distrust.

The "peace of God, which passeth all understanding" can be yours (Philippians 4:7). All of us desire to have peace. We look for it in college degrees, marriages, friendships, where we live, careers—in everything but God our creator. God is the author and giver of peace. When your life has been surrendered to God and His will, you learn to rest in the confidence of His ability and wait for His plans to be carried out as He desires.

This book, coupled with the Bible, will take you on an attainable journey toward transformation, peace, and contentment. This will serve as a catalyst for you, as you live in a sinful and self-centered world. This book will show you how to move when you've felt paralyzed. You will gain the strength to obtain rest when you have been weary. You will be given the tools to live with a higher perspective. You will learn the power of positive thinking while enduring trials and tribulations. You will be able to exhibit stamina while running the race, moving toward the life God has planned for you.

I pray that every reader of this book and the Bible will draw closer to God as He waits to be our friend and the driving force in our lives. May God's plan for His glorification be carried out through each of us. Let your journey begin. Great things await you!

Section One

Honesty With Self is the Best Policy

Chapter 1
A Look On the Inside

Alcoholics will never seek help until they accept that they are alcoholics. Selfish persons can never receive help until they acknowledge their selfishness. A depressed mother can never get better until she admits there is a problem. A troubled marriage cannot improve until both individuals take responsibility for themselves.

Honesty: to be truthful, to not lie or cheat, to open your heart for truth. God wants us to be honest with ourselves, so we can heal on the inside. The strength to change comes from God. We can easily make changes to our physical appearance by coloring our hair when we see gray; throwing away our glasses after vision correction surgery; or dieting to lose weight.

 Honesty: to be truthful, to not lie or cheat, to open your heart for truth.

The real test is when we attempt and struggle with changing our inner woman. A woman's soul is a valuable and priceless possession. As we grow from children into adults, life brings us challenges. We may have had alcoholic parents, been abused, or remember being cold or hungry. Our fathers or mothers may have abandoned us. We might have had everything we desired but never felt loved. Life can be very cruel over time, and we become products of our environment. If our household was loving, we learned to show love. If our home was chaotic, we learned to be frustrated. If our home was discouraging, we learned to be critical. The beauty of looking at ourselves is that we find answers for why we behave certain ways. These actions may be positive or negative. However, in exposing ourselves we learn our weaknesses and can grow in patience toward others.

I have met many people who have allowed the challenges of life to make them miserable and frustrated about every little thing. These types of people always look for the negative and believe their situations are far worse than anyone else's. By looking on the inside and going to God with our frustrations, hurts, and pains, we can learn how to have joy. Our finances may not be good, our health may be failing, and we may have lost loved ones. But as we learn to seek God fervently with a pure heart, we learn that God has the ability to help us.

"But I have prayed for thee, that thy faith fail not" (Luke 22:32a). We may not realize the love that God has for us, and we may take it for granted. "Nor height, nor depth, nor any other creature, shall be able to separate us from the love of God, which is in Christ Jesus our Lord" (Romans 8:39). Absolutely nothing can separate us from the love of God. He hates sin, but He loves us despite our disobedience.

God Can Only Use Me When I'm Honest

Have you ever wondered why God made you? Do you want your life to have meaning and purpose? We must continually surrender to God. He has many plans for us. He wants to use us to save the lost. "The spirit of the Lord is upon me, because he hath anointed me to preach the gospel to the poor; he hath sent me to heal the brokenhearted, to preach deliverance to the captives, and recovering of sight to the blind, to set at liberty them that are bruised" (Luke 4:18).

When we are honest with God and ourselves, we can minister to people. There are thousands of lost souls looking for an answer to the cares and troubles of this life. The only way the world will ever be able to see God is through faithful Christians. We can give answers to those in despair by talking about the difficulties from which God has delivered us. This is one of the reasons we have trials. What would we have to share with others if we never had challenges in our lives?

"Now then we are ambassadors [ones who go on errands] for Christ" (2 Corinthians 5:20). Psalms 51:1–19 shows David humbly pouring his heart out to God for sinning with Bathsheba and having her husband killed. God was able to call David "a man after His own heart" (1 Samuel 13:14). David had an honest and sincere heart, and he knew that his sinful choice cost him his relationship with God. David had established respect for God as a boy, and he increased his faith through believing and witnessing God's power. This was evident as he (with God's help) killed a lion and a bear (17:34–37). He went on to kill Goliath when all others believed the giant could not be defeated. Once again, David was confident in God's power and believed that He would assist him.

The beauty of David's repentance was the fact that he had experienced God and His power through rough times. God loves a humble heart. Jesus exhibited this when He went to the cross. "[N]evertheless not as I will, but as thou wilt" (Matthew 26:39). "[M]an looketh on the outward appearance, but the LORD looketh on the heart" (1 Samuel 16:7). Changing our physical appearance is easy, but the true test comes when we must make changes within ourselves.

Changing our physical appearance is easy, but the true test comes when we must make changes within ourselves.

"Examine yourselves whether ye be in the faith; prove your own selves" (2 Corinthians 13:5). We don't like to talk about those things. We may need to admit that we are liars, gossips, prideful, materialistic, jealous, or hateful. However, admitting these things to God or having others tell us certain things about ourselves does not feel good. But if we sincerely desire to please God it must be done! God already knows our flaws and weaknesses; but when we acknowledge them, God sees our humble and genuine hearts.

Who Am I?

The moment God begins to form us in the womb, we are under His protection. "I will praise thee; for I am fearfully and wonderfully made: marvellous are thy works; and that my soul knoweth right well" (Psalm 139:14). "But the very hairs of your head are all numbered" (Matthew 10:30). God formed and protected us while we were in the womb. We did not arrive here by chance. Our mothers' care for themselves played its part, but ultimately it was God (the giver of life) who brought us into the world. God knows everything about us. Being honest with God frees us to accept our baggage and humbly ask God through prayer to help us in our weaknesses.

Choosing Not To Be Honest With Self

Once we make up our minds to live with blinders on, God cannot use us for His purpose. How was honesty handled in your home as a child? Were you told to keep secrets? Were you not allowed to show emotion or speak about your true feelings? Were you popular, or were you teased in school? Do you feel like a bad mother when you are unable to give your child all he or she may want? When you have a spat with your husband, do you retreat and pretend everything is okay? Do you desire for everybody to like you? Do you have difficulty telling your friends when they are wrong? How you answer these thought-provoking questions is a direct result of how you perceive being honest about who you truly are.

When we choose not to deal with our past and shortcomings, we run the risk of habitually practicing self-destructive behaviors. We can't live in the present and be successful if we are carrying excess baggage. The decisions we make today will be made based upon our past. How can God use us if we are running from Him? We only improve when we confront our weaknesses and struggles. God knows and sees all things. Christianity is not just going through the motions of rituals and traditions, but living a peaceable life of servanthood—flaws and all.

When we choose not to be honest with ourselves, we are living a lie. We drift through life aimlessly. I call it living on "Fantasy Island." The wife who refuses to admit she is having marital problems leaves the impression that her marriage is okay—until an affair is made public. The mother who believes her child can do no wrong upholds that child in his or her bad choices. The woman who marries multiple times in hopes of finding "Mr. Right" refuses to consider what need she is attempting to fulfill. Every time we refuse to be honest with ourselves, we take a step backward.

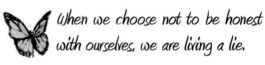 *When we choose not to be honest with ourselves, we are living a lie.*

By the same token, dishonesty with God leaves us with a false sense of fulfillment, and we practice self-centered behaviors. Our Christian life then consists of being served rather than serving others. We may choose to marry people who do not have relationships with God. We convince ourselves that they are faithful and jump the broom for a false sense of marital bliss. We take a job for the mega-bucks only, although it requires us to work Sundays. We choose friendships that feed our fleshly appetites. We remain close friends with those who encourage us to dislike our spouses, be motherless to our children and not get involved with church work. The sermons heard become words for others, and we avoid looking at ourselves.

This lifestyle keeps us hijacked spiritually. We strive to please ourselves and have no time for God. The one we are really working for is Satan. He has us where he wants us. "Satan hath desired to have you, that he may sift you as wheat" (Luke 22:31). When we are all about pleasing ourselves, our children suffer. Our marriages become war zones. We are not examples but rather hindrances to the lost. We seek to fulfill the pleasures of the world. "He that is not with me is against me" (Matthew 12:30). "No man can serve two masters: for either will hate the one, and love the other; or else he will hold to the one, and despise the other. Ye cannot serve God and mammon [money]" (Matthew 6:24).

King Nebuchadnezzar refused to humble himself and worship God. God made him like a beast. He grew hair like eagles' feathers, his nails became as birds' claws and he ate grass. He remained in this state for seven years of his life (Daniel 4:32, 33).

In Exodus 7–12, Pharaoh refused to let the children of Israel leave Egypt, and God sent plagues upon the Egyptians. Because of his pride, Pharaoh continued to harden his heart. A rebellious heart does not prosper but only moves toward self-destruction. "The fear of the LORD is to hate evil: pride, and arrogancy, and the evil way, and the froward [stubbornly disobedient] mouth, do I hate" (Proverbs 8:13). "Pride goeth before destruction, and an haughty spirit before a fall" (Proverbs 16:18).

How Do I See Myself?

We may be suffering from low self-esteem and find it hard to tell someone else he or she looks nice. We may be having financial difficulties and cannot rejoice with friends who buy new homes. We may suffer from discontentment, so we buy every new thing that comes out, giving no thought for how we will pay for it. We may have past pain from a tragic childhood, and we find it hard to be kind to others. We may believe that we have to purchase the best of everything, because we grew up poor. We have bought into what the world considers success—the type of cars we drive, designer-only clothing, the neighborhoods we choose to live in, and the types of jobs we have. If these things make us feel better about who we are, then we will never be fulfilled. "[R]iches certainly make themselves wings; they fly away as an eagle toward heaven" (Proverbs 23:5).

I'm certainly not saying that having things is necessarily bad. However, if we are more focused on acquiring man's standard of success, hoping this will give us peace, we have totally missed the point. Success for Christians is to develop the desire for our ways to please God. (Proverbs 16:7, Psalms 119:5)

Worldly success can be deceitful; we get caught up in it sometimes. Man seeks happiness in a spouse, joy in a child, or pleasure in a new home. All of these things are temporary. Peace can only be found in God. A husband's purpose is not to make his wife happy. Only God can fulfill and complete her. She should not expect her spouse to fulfill her. God did not create humans for that purpose. Humans make mistakes and cause hurt sometimes. If we are surrendering to God, our spouses only enhance what God has already put into us.

If we are looking for our children to give us joy, what happens when they choose a college or profession that we may not like? What is our reaction when they make bad choices and lose their direction for a time? Do we practice forgiveness? Do we withhold love from them? Children are to be reared to be given back to God. We do our best to live Christian lives sincerely before them and teach them at home who God is. We do all that we can to ensure that they have the opportunities and support they need to be successful. Ultimately, it's up to them to choose the road they want to travel.

Do material possessions hold you hostage? It's important to acknowledge that they are only a temporary fix. They are not meant to last. What happens when the car is no longer new or the house no longer has the newest gadgets? What if you are unable to pay the mortgage because of health problems? We should be more concerned about our prayer lives and how much time we are spending meditating on God's Word. Are we preparing ourselves for the challenges of life through daily Bible study, meditation, and application of God's Word? We must create substance in our lives by realizing that we belong to God.

In 1 Peter 2:9 we read that we are "a chosen generation, a royal priesthood, an holy nation, a peculiar people." We are called to be different. "Wherefore come out from among them, and be ye separate" (2 Corinthians 6:17). We need to be a generation of Christians that humbly gives biblical direction to the lost. Let us be Christian parents that are engulfing our children with the Word of God. The only way the world sees our Heavenly Father is through His children. The world needs us to be examples in our marriages, in rearing our children, or in practicing abstinence as single Christians. We show other women how to love their husbands and children by practicing *agape* love within our families. We must buy into Jesus and not the world's standards of peace and joy.

"But whoso looketh into the perfect law of liberty, and continueth therein, he being not a forgetful hearer, but a doer of the work, this man shall be blessed in his deed" (James 1:25). How many of us look in the mirror before walking out the door to make sure we are presentable? We wouldn't go anywhere in our pajamas or with our hair uncombed. We are quick to put on the wonderful smells of perfume and lotions. We have our nails manicured and our teeth whitened. Do we spend more time looking in the mirror each day than we spend studying God's Word? What is more important?

Each day we must look into God's Word and compare our lives, in speech, attitude, and thought, with what the Bible teaches. We must take the time to ask ourselves, "What makes us tick?" "What demands our time?" "Do we seek to please God or man?" James encourages us to make the necessary changes so that we can meet God's face in peace. We can only develop the desire to be clothed in righteousness when we are seeking to please God. Ephesians 6 tells us the type of clothing to wear: "Put on the whole armour of God, that ye may be able to stand against the wiles of the devil" (v. 11). "Wherefore take unto you the whole armour of God, that ye may be able to withstand in the evil day, and having done, all to stand" (v. 13). Our enemy is Satan. We must wear our spiritual armor daily so that we can recognize Satan's evil devices and defeat him!

Focusing On What Others See

Seeking to make sure that our physical appearance meets man's standards drives us to work only on our outward appearance. It's easier to work on the outer appearance. We can mask inner pain with new cars. We can hide hurt with new dresses. We can hide physical abuse with sweaters or sunglasses. We can point fingers at others when we don't want to see our own flaws. We can attend worship and pretend the messages are for someone else. We can mask the painfulness of divorce by blaming our spouses. The energy and time we spend trying to look good for others is costly.

Saying the right things publicly is easier than admitting our weaknesses. We learn to keep our real hurts inside, and we become bitter. We have more stress when we hide our shortcomings. We never can have the abundant lives that God wants for us (John 10:10). Peace can never be ours. The more we work on our outward appearances, the farther we move from God. We feel safe when we don't sincerely look at ourselves. Staying in our comfort zone is what we are used to. The challenge is moving away from that zone, and seeking the transformation process that God has in store for us.

Developing a Willingness to Change

Do we want more from our Christianity? Do we want to have the faith that is required to sustain us? Do we want to have true peace? Are we tired of temporary fixes? Are we tired of doing the same routines and getting the same negative results? Then we must grow sick and tired of the direction our lives are headed.

Real courage and growth comes when we can honestly examine ourselves based upon the Word of God. These moments of self-evaluation lead us closer to God, and we develop humble spirits. During this time of learning and admitting our weaknesses, we develop powerful relationships with God, our creator.

We ask God for strength to forgive the unforgivable. We ask God for courage to walk through the fires of change. We ask God for stamina when we go through fleshly withdrawals. Change is very painful, because we are asking God to change our thought processes. We may have had these thoughts for years, but

Real courage and growth comes when we can honestly examine ourselves based upon the Word of God.

when we become Christians these thoughts don't go away—they become stronger.

The first piece to the puzzle is to repent. We must have willing minds (2 Corinthians 8:12). We acknowledge the sin in our lives to God and ask for help to "put off the old man with his deeds" (Colossians 3:9).

The second piece is having the faith to know that God wants to make us better. We must believe that God is all powerful and can heal us. God's plan is to fill that void with His divine Word. God, in His infinite wisdom, has given us everything we need to follow Him. "Let this mind be in you, which was also in Christ Jesus" (Philippians 2:5). To develop the mind of Christ, we must allow God to speak to us through His Word as we speak to God through prayer.

"Faith is what makes real the things we hope for. It is proof of what we cannot see" (Hebrews 11:1 *ERV*). We know that God is real by looking at all the beautiful things He created. Our faith is enhanced as we study and apply His Word. Our hope is in going to heaven and knowing that God is everywhere and sees all things. We learn to appreciate and look forward to the coming of Christ. We acknowledge there is life after death, and we long for eternal life. Once we begin to experience God through consistent relationships with Him, we rest in the knowledge that the changes He is able to make in our lives are for our benefit.

"But without faith it is impossible to please him: for he that cometh to God must believe that he is, and that he is a rewarder of them that diligently seek him" (Hebrews 11:6). Our first desire must be to please God through believing who He is and what He can do.

Are You Flying Solo?

"O LORD, I know that the way of man is not in himself: it is not in man that walketh to direct his steps" (Jeremiah 10:23). Are you flying solo? Do you believe you can go through this process alone? Change is a must. So often we are willing to change jobs, move to

other states or make new friends; but we are unwilling to make changes in ourselves.

If we have the desire to change, we have to accept the Bible as the divine Word of God. The Bible is our road map from earth to heaven. The Bible contains everything we need to learn about managing our money, being good wives, rearing our children, selecting professions, or choosing mates. The Bible will help us to think before we react. It will give us peace in the midst of our storms. God's Word will strengthen us in our weaknesses and will calm our restless spirit. "Sanctify [to dedicate, make holy] them through thy truth: thy word is truth" (John 17:17).

> Most important of all, you must understand this: No prophecy [teaching or message from God] in the Scriptures [holy writings] comes from the prophet's own understanding. No prophecy ever came from what some person wanted to say. But people were led by the Holy Spirit and spoke words from God. (2 Peter 1:20, 21, *ERV*).

Change is a lifelong process. We should strive to repent and put forth the efforts to draw closer to God. We are preparing now for our final destination (Matthew 25:1–12). God wants to find us busy in His work—teaching the lost, encouraging the saved, striving to obey His Word, and preparing daily to see His face—as we await His Son's return (Matthew 25:13).

As we practice denying ourselves, let us examine ourselves daily with God's Word and repent of those things that are hindering us from reaching our goal. "Let us hear the conclusion of the whole matter: Fear God, and keep his commandments: for this is the whole duty of man" (Ecclesiastes 12:13).

Open Your Bible, Grab a Pen and Paper.

1. Memorize 2 Corinthians 13:5. Write the verse on a colored index card. Place the card in your purse, on your refrigerator, or attach it to your bathroom mirror.
2. Make a list of what you like about yourself. Make a list of what you dislike and want to change.
3. Make a list of your sins and how they are hindering you spiritually.
4. What is the definition of a reprobate?
5. Finish this sentence: I'll do better when _____.
6. Memorize and meditate on 2 Corinthians 8:12. List three ways this Scripture can help you be useful for God.
7. What baggage from your past has you held hostage? What can you do to overcome it?

Application

Invite a sister that you would like to get to know better to your house for lunch or out to lunch this week.

Ask for help from a faithful Christian woman who can encourage you toward spiritual maturity.

Write a list of spiritual goals that you would like to accomplish. Develop a plan to put those goals into action.

Chapter 2
Forgetting Those Things

Once we decide that we are going to seek transformation, we must do what Philippians 3:12, 13 says:

> I don't mean that I am exactly what God wants me to be. I have not yet reached that goal. But I continue trying to reach it and make it mine. That's what Christ Jesus wants me to do. It is the reason he made me his. Brothers and sisters, I know that I still have a long way to go. But there is one thing I do: I forget what is in the past and try as hard as I can to reach the goal before me (*ERV*).

We must begin to forgive ourselves for the things we have done in the past. We must resolve to seek peace and transformation against our past; this will lead us toward inner renewal. "For which cause we faint not; but though our outward man perish, yet the inward man is renewed day by day" (2 Corinthians 4:16). We must renew our spirits daily by studying God's Word and meditating on worthwhile things.

Our Past Can Be a Blessing or a Curse

"And such were some of you: but ye are washed, but ye are sanctified, but ye are justified in the name of the Lord Jesus, and by the spirit of our God" (1 Corinthians 6:11). Many of us have come to God having been unrighteous, fornicators, idolaters, adulterers, thieves, and drunkards (vv. 9, 10). The road of life may have taken us to places we thought we would never be. We may have made choices to please our-selves, or we may have made choices in ignorance.

We must make up in our minds to follow God by obeying the gospel of Jesus Christ. We must strive to be faithful unto death (Revelation 2:10). Jesus forgives us our past sins at baptism, and the gift of the Holy Spirit is given to assist us in navigating through life. Our old behaviors do not go away, but we are more equipped to deal with them. Once we are baptized the real work begins. We must make conscious efforts no longer to be in Satan's army but to be soldiers for Christ.

Our spiritual warfare has begun, and Satan just declared war on us. Do we panic? Do we run in fear? When the challenges of our past en-tice us to go back to our old ways, we have choices to make (Proverbs 1:10). Do we follow God or follow man? The help that God gives us through understanding His Word will enable us to choose rightly. By not studying the Bible we feed our old ways, and we may be influenced to do evil. We won't make the mark every time; but as long as God sees us trying, His grace (unmerited favor) covers us.

God requires us to make a conscious effort to follow Him. Satan wants us to allow our past choices to derail us. As certain topics are discussed in Bible classes, we may begin to feel worthless and shame-ful. We must realize that God has forgiven us of our sins and washed them away with the blood of Jesus. Satan uses the oldest trick in the book; if he can get us to see ourselves as small and unforgivable, he can continue to lead us toward self-blame.

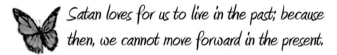 *Satan loves for us to live in the past; because then, we cannot move forward in the present.*

Satan loves for us to live in the past; because then, we cannot move forward in the present. Satan wants us to become stalled, derailed and hopeless. This is like running in place or going nowhere fast. God does not want us to run in place; but to run the race that is set before us with zeal, courage, and security in knowing that God is with us (He-

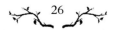

brews 12:1, 2). He has promised, "I will never leave thee, nor forsake thee. So that we may boldly say, The Lord is my helper, and I will not fear what man shall do unto me" (Hebrews 13:5b, 6).

Out With the Old, In With the New

The biggest thing that helps me to forgive myself when I sin is to write my sins down, read them aloud, repent, and ask God to help me. I keep a dated prayer and study journal, which helps me to evaluate the things that are contributing to my falls spiritually. I ask myself these questions: "Am I allowing negative influences in my life?" or "Do I need courage to stand for what is right?"

My next step is to locate and research Scriptures that pertain to my sins. The last step is throwing the list of sins in the trashcan. I pray specifically for help to overcome them. I know by asking God for help that He will send tests, so I can grow in these areas of weakness.

Satan does not want us to acknowledge our sins to God; He wants us to continue negative self-talk. We tend to think on statements such as these: "I can never be faithful!"; "This is too hard!"; "Why can't I do what I want?"; "I'm not hurting anyone!"; "No one will ever find out!"; or "If they would just help me do right!" This thought process will cause us to make excuses for our choices and never get better. What if Jesus had that mindset when God sent Him to earth?

Still in the Self-Hatred Mode

When we don't give our failures to God, we cannot learn to forgive ourselves. Our self-hate mindset adopts habits of unhappiness, depression, anger, and presumptuous sins. We become unproductive in rearing our children or being good wives and friends. We have difficulty rejoicing with others, enjoying our lives, and living peaceful and joy-filled existences. There is so much power in self-forgiveness. We realize that we are not perfect. We keep trying, by the grace of God, re-

When we don't give our failures to God, we cannot learn to forgive ourselves.

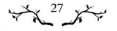

gardless of being mentally tired. We stay focused on our goals and accept God's unconditional love.

Once we accept God's forgiveness, we are free to live abundant lives. Obedience to God leads to joy. When we do things to satisfy our wants, we are moving toward despair and self-destruction.

Take Up Your Bed and Walk

The Scriptures tell us to pick up our stuff, admit it, and move on. This is especially true when our sins are recalled to us continually from those closest to us. Satan enjoys this; because for that moment our minds go back to the wrongs we have done. If we are not careful to clear our minds, we will be back in the modes of self-hate. Knowing God for ourselves can free us from dwelling on the negative reminders that people use against us .Satan wants us to think that our sins are too big for God to forgive. Decide to make the devil mad by forgiving yourself, and make God glad by accepting His forgiveness.

> Who shall separate us from the love of Christ? shall tribulation, or distress, or persecution, or famine, or nakedness, or peril, or sword? As it is written, For thy sake we are killed all the day long; we are accounted as sheep for the slaughter. Nay, in all these things we are more than conquerors through him that loved us. For I am persuaded, that neither death, nor life, nor angels, nor principalities, nor powers, nor things present, nor things to come, Nor height, nor depth, nor any other creature, shall be able to separate us from the love of God, which is in Christ Jesus our Lord (Romans 8:35–39).

God's love is constant and forever. His love never changes. God loves us during our difficulties, and He is walking alongside us when we cannot see our way. He is with us when we are being challenged. He is guiding us through the maze when we feel our footsteps slipping.

I have heard so many people say, "I'll get baptized when I get myself right." We can't heal without God. "For all have sinned, and come short of the glory of God" (Romans 3:23). We see God's love through Him sending His Son, Jesus, to die for our sins (John 3:16).

"What shall we say then? Shall we continue in sin, that grace may abound? God forbid. How shall we, that are dead to sin, live any longer therein?" (Romans 6:1, 2). We can't sin willfully on a continual basis and expect His grace to continue. God wants us putting forth a moment-by-moment effort to do the right thing. He must find us working on our weaknesses. "If ye love me, keep my commandments" (John 14:15). God's unselfishness is magnificent! He wants each of us to love Him with all our heart, soul, and might (Deuteronomy 6:5). Why wouldn't He want our love and devotion? He gave the ultimate sacrifice! We would not want to give our children to die to save people that we do not know. Would our faith be as strong as Abraham's? He humbly surrendered and almost killed his own son in obedience to God's request. God saw Abraham's devotion to Him, and the angel of the Lord told Abraham not to harm his son (Genesis 22:1–13).

I'm not saying we need to sacrifice our children, but I am saying that our allegiance to God should be our first priority and desire. We cannot change our past, but we can accept each new day that God gives us. Make the choice to be faithful today. We need to practice the art of forgiving ourselves daily as we repent of our sins.

Open Your Bible, Grab a Pen and Paper.

1. What does it mean to move forward?
2. List the areas in which you are having difficulty forgiving yourself. Beside each of the areas listed, give steps toward resolving these problems. On your list, draw an X through all of the things you cannot change.

3. What are some negative things you say to yourself? How can you learn to change your thoughts? Locate a Scripture to counter each negative thought.
4. How can your past become a blessing to others?
5. Write a prayer to God about forgiving yourself.

 *Application*

Memorize Philippians 4:8, 9 and Psalm 119:59, 60.

Resolve to live in the present—one step at a time.
Make it a practice as soon as your eyes open each morning
to pray to God.

Chapter 3
Come out With Your Hands Up

*I*n the middle of the night, imagine being awakened by a loud banging on your door. As you open the door, you are met by blue flashing lights and a police officer saying, "Come out with your hands up!" This is what comes to my mind when God calls us to be obedient to His Word. While your hands are up in the air, you say, "I give up; you've got me." The only way that we can become obedient is to realize that we need God. We need to say, "I'm no longer going to try to do this life by myself." We must face the reality of the bad choices we've made and the consequences we've suffered for those decisions.

> And he said to them all, If any man will come after me, let him deny himself, and take up his cross daily, and follow me. For whosoever will save his life shall lose it: but whosoever will lose his life for my sake, the same shall save it (Luke 9:23, 24).

Surrender: to give up, to yield possession or power. Jesus is saying that when we decide to follow Him we must deny ourselves. We must give up what we want. Everything we do has to be approved by God. If it isn't, we cannot involve ourselves in it. Self-denial is a deliberate daily choice. Every day we will be faced with the challenges to follow God or do what we want. We may be asked by co-workers on a Wednesday night to go out for drinks after work. Do we go for drinks or go to Bible class? We face a myriad of choices between good and evil every day. Some of these tests we will pass, and some we will fail. A consistent study of God's Word is the only thing that can help us make the proper choices. Once we become soldiers for Christ, we agree to be partakers in suffering for the cause of Christ (1 Peter 4:13).

This may mean that our families will distance themselves, because they may not agree with our choice to follow God. We may lose friends because we choose not to participate in the activities we used to do. We may be ridiculed by people that know or don't know us. We may experience teasing from those who should love us.

If we give up our wants and desires, we will find our purpose in life. God will be able to use us. We will experience peace by being obedient to God. If we try to hold on to our wants and desires, we will lose our lives. We will go through our lives frustrated, and our choices will not please God. Therefore, we will not benefit and will be hindered by them.

 If we give up our wants and desires, we will find our purpose in life.

God is not asking us to do something impossible (Luke 9:23, 24). We must fight daily to do what is right. As we make positive choices, we grow spiritually. As the battles become harder, we get tougher.

Jesus is our prime example. From the time he was 12 years old, He was about His Father's business (Luke 2:49); we must be that self-disciplined. The choices that we make to follow God are for our betterment. Following our Heavenly Father keeps us from walking into trouble. We serve God in thankfulness for all He has done. We obey God because we love Him. We must allow the Bible to speak to us. Let us not harden our hearts. "Happy is the man that feareth alway: but he that hardeneth his heart shall fall into mischief" (Proverbs 28:14).

A Living Sacrifice

I beseech you therefore, brethren, by the mercies of God, that ye present your bodies a living sacrifice, holy, acceptable unto God, which is your reasonable service. And be not conformed to this world: but be ye transformed by the renewing of your mind, that ye may prove what is that good, and acceptable, and perfect, will of God (Romans 12:1, 2).

We must present our lives as gifts to God for all the kindness and unselfishness He has shown to us. We do this through obedience to His Word. When we put this into practice, we strive to please God and not man. We don't worry when we are mistreated or ridiculed, because we are only concerned with pleasing God.

The only way we can develop a new way of thinking is by studying and applying God's Word. If we are struggling with jealousy, we should look in the Scriptures for resolution. If we cannot seem to forgive those who have wronged us, we should search for examples of a forgiving spirit shown in the Bible. As we begin to look for answers to our problems, we are comforted by God's instruction. The pleasures of the world will draw our appetites at various times. If we fill our hearts (minds) with God's Word through wisdom (James 1:5), we see the dangers of partaking in "the pleasures of sin for a season" (Hebrews 11:25).

When we allow ourselves to be pulled back into the passions of the world, we should discipline ourselves and bring ourselves back "into subjection." After we have preached to others, we do not want to be castaways (1 Corinthians 9:27). As we surrender to God's Word we find direction. The crooked road becomes straight. We learn where to look for and accept peace. We learn to acknowledge and do what God would have us to do. We know He is working to make us better.

Who Is Great Among You?

Have you ever met anyone famous? Do you know someone who has met a famous person? He or she is usually very eager to tell everybody they know about it. The most famous person we could ever meet is Jesus Christ. "But it shall not be so among you: but whosoever will be great among you, let him be your minister; And whosoever will be chief among you, let him be your servant: Even as the Son of man came not to be ministered unto, but to minister, and to give his life a ransom for many" (Matthew 20:26–28).

The world's standard of greatness goes to the man at the top of the corporate ladder. Often he is not the one who gets his hands dirty or performs menial tasks. But God says His standard of greatness goes to the man who can serve others. The woman who can walk in another woman's shoes is truly the great one.

> In your lives you must think and act like Christ Jesus. Christ Himself was like God in everything. Christ was equal with God. But Christ did not think that being equal with God was something that he must keep. He gave up His place with God and agreed to be like a servant. He was born to be a man and became like a servant. And he was living as a man he humbled himself by being fully obedient to God. He obeyed even when that caused him to die on the cross. Christ obeyed God, so God raised Christ to the most important place. God made the name of Christ greater than every other name (Philippians 2:5–9, *ERV*).

God in His infinite wisdom gave us direction for our motives in doing His work.

> Be careful when you do good things, don't do those things in front of people. Don't do those things for people to see you. If you do that, then you will have no reward from your Father in heaven. When you give to poor people don't announce that you are giving. Don't do like the hypocrites do. They blow trumpets before they give so that people will see them. They do that in the synagogues and on the streets. They want other people to give honor to them. So when you give to poor people, give very secretly. Don't let any person know what you are doing. Your giving should be done in secret. Your Father

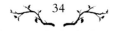

can see the things that are done in secret. And he will reward you (Matthew 6:1–4, *ERV*).

We should come out with our hands up and be transformed toward a better life. Not to just live, but to live peacefully and to be an example to others as they see us struggle. Not to just be okay, but to be victorious because of Whose we are.

Open Your Bible, Grab a Pen and Paper,

1. What does it mean to deny yourself?
2. Write down what you need to give up to follow God.
3. Is giving up certain things difficult for you? If so, why?
4. How can your life be a living sacrifice?
5. What does it mean to be servant? What are some good works you can become involved in at your congregation?
6. How do you know what God wants for you?
7. If you know what God wants for you, how can you practice humility while still using your talents?

Application

Ask to teach a Bible class for the age group
you feel most comfortable working with.

Consider hosting a ladies' devotional luncheon in your home.
Ask the attendees to bring their favorite Scripture for discussion.

Section Two

The Jackhammer

Chapter 4
Counting the Cost

B y faith Noah, being warned of God of things not seen as yet, moved with fear, prepared an ark to the saving of his house; by the which he condemned the world, and became heir of the righteousness which is by faith" (Hebrews 11:7). Noah could've said "no," but he did as God requested and was saved from death. In 2 Kings 5:1-14, we read of Naaman and his sickness with leprosy. Naaman was told to dip in the Jordan River seven times, but he refused (vv. 11, 12). He had his own idea of how he should be healed. Through the persuasion of his servants, Naaman decided to follow the instructions of Elisha. He went to dip into the Jordan River and was healed (vv. 13, 14). The cost of not going to the Jordan would have been a life with leprosy. In Luke 4:27, we read that Naaman was the only leper healed in Israel in the time of Elisha.

We have the tools to build a strong Christian life. "Except the LORD build the house, they labour in vain that build it: except the LORD keep the city, the watchman waketh but in vain" (Psalm 127:1). If we are not surrendering to God for guidance, then all that we are doing is in vain (useless).

Paul was a persecutor of the church and eventually ended up being an important part of the very thing he had persecuted. "At one time all these things were important to me. But because of Christ, I decided that they are worth nothing. Not only these things, but now I think that all things are worth nothing compared with the greatness of knowing Christ Jesus my Lord" (Philippians 3:7, 8, *ERV*). Paul is saying that at one time his passion was persecuting the church. Once he chose to follow God, he realized all of his previous endeavors were worthless and self-absorbed. He had been driven by his own desires. He came to the resolution that knowing God was more valuable.

What Is Required of Me?

If we truly desire to follow Christ we must ask ourselves, what does God require of us? What are the things that we need to give up for God?

We often view following God with a narrow perspective. We think that choosing to become a Christian is or will become boring. We may see lives that are rigid and strict. We may spend more time planning and saving for summer vacations than we do planning to follow God.

> If you wanted to build a building, you would first sit down and decide how much it would cost. You must see if you have enough money to finish the job. If you don't do that, you might begin the work, but you would not be able to finish. And if you could not finish it, everyone would laugh at you. They would say, "This man began to build, but he was not able to finish!" If a king is going to fight against another king, first he will sit down and plan. If the king has only 10,000 men, he will try to decide if he is able to defeat the other king who has 20,000 men. If he thinks he cannot defeat the other king, he will send some men to ask for peace while that king's army is still far away. It is the same for each of you. You must leave everything you have to follow me. If not, you cannot be my follower! (Luke 14:28–33, *ERV*).

We must take inventory of the things that are hindering us from following God and decide if these things are worth holding onto. To follow God takes self-denial and effort. God has every right to ask that we give up everything we have to follow Him. He willingly developed a plan for our salvation through giving up His Son for us. Christ is our example of giving up self, and we see God as lovingly sacrificial. Christ had everything He needed, but He obeyed His Father and came to the world and became as we are. He went through every human emotion that we have, yet He stayed on course to do the will of His Father. As He surrendered to that cruel death on the cross, He said "Father, forgive them; for they know not what they do" (Luke 23:34).

 God has every right to ask that we give up everything we have to follow Him.

Matthew 10:37 tells us if a person loves his father, mother, son or daughter more than God, he or she is not worthy of Him. Jesus says, "A man's foes [enemies] shall be they of his own household" (v. 36). Once we decide to follow God, many times our challenges come from our own households rather than from any other source. Our lives as Christians may not be accepted by our families. The non-Christian husband may seek ways to influence his Christian wife not to attend worship. The young adult Christian may be encouraged by unfaithful parents to not be involved in ministry work. The teenage Christian could be living with a drug-addicted mother and an abusive father making it difficult to serve God. These situations, as well as countless others, can be lethal to hinder us on our journeys. A faithful church striving to do right can be a huge support system to those being devoured by their physical families. God gives us a new family in Christ Jesus. "When my father and mother forsake me, then the LORD will take me up" (Psalm 27:10). Christianity is not easy; nor is it a walk in the park. It is an all-day discipline to follow God. God only requires us to put forth the effort and not faint. "And let us not be weary in well doing: for in due season we shall reap, if we faint not" (Galatians 6:9).

I am always encouraged when I see a young mother bringing her children to church in spite of her tiredness. I am encouraged when a young teenager is present in Bible class regardless of the ridicule she suffers from her physical family. I am uplifted when I see a fellow church member who I know suffers with severe headaches, and she's one of the first ones sitting on the pew. When we are in the state of denying ourselves, this is when God can really use us. The family members that ridicule the teenage girl can be influenced for good by her faithfulness. They may eventually decide to attend worship service and obey the gospel. The young Christian mother will someday see the fruits of her sacrificial labor as she watches her children get baptized and lead faithful lives. The member with chronic headaches may never know how many people she has encouraged to be faithful. The reality is, once we surrender to God He uses our joys and sorrows to lead the lost to Him; and He is glorified. We can bring the thoughts of heaven into each day that God gives us. "For the Lord himself shall descend from heaven with a shout, with the voice of the archangel, and with the trump of God: and the dead in Christ shall rise first: Then we which are alive and remain shall be caught up together with them in the clouds, to meet the Lord in the air: and so shall we ever be with the Lord. Wherefore comfort one another with these words" (1 Thessalonians 4:16–18).

The reality is, once we surrender to God He uses our joys and sorrows to lead the lost to Him; and he is glorified.

God requires us to study and meditate upon His Word and apply it to our lives. This is part of counting the cost. How much time are we willing to give up to grow spiritually? Do we miss some sleep and rise early to meditate on His Word? Do we add God to our to-do lists? Is He included in our vacation plans? The only way we can know the direction God wants us to go is by allowing Him to speak to us through His Word.

"Study to shew thyself approved unto God, a workman that needeth not to be ashamed, rightly dividing the word of truth" (2 Timothy 2:15). As we study God's Word we grow spiritually, and we are able to boldly and humbly tell others the truth of God's Word in the correct ways.

When we choose to study, this allows the world to see how God is impacting our lives. Many of us may have been liars, adulterers, thieves, and fornicators. The humility in obeying God is that the old sinful part of our lives becomes a testimony for the lost, the disheartened and the weary. Our learning of God's Word creates a relationship with Him. We don't deliberately involve ourselves in sinful practices when we feel the urge to do so. We don't pursue other people's spouses to fulfill our desires. We don't steal, because God commands that we work with our hands to have the things we need. Singles practice abstinence and avoid situations that will arouse their sexual desires. We all grow in humility and service to God.

We must meditate upon what we have studied. To meditate means to contemplate and think. When we mediate on God's Word we repeat it and memorize it. We pray to God to fully understand and grasp what He is trying to teach us. This is when the Scriptures come to life. I can recall times when I have searched the Scriptures to find an answer on something I'm struggling with. The relief and serenity that I receive from particular passages is always humbling. "According to his divine power hath given unto us all things that pertain unto life and godliness" (2 Peter 1:3). We just have to be willing to pick up our Bibles and expect to receive something every time we study. The biggest thing that helps me to remember what I have studied is to write it down. "O how love I thy law! it is my meditation all the day … Thy word is a lamp unto my feet, and a light unto my path" (Psalm 119:97, 105).

How can God's Word become our meditation "all the day"? I suggest keeping an index card file of Scriptures that you study. The blessings of having access to a Bible throughout the day can help tremendously. You may consider having a Bible in your car, bathroom, other areas throughout your home, in your purse, or in your desk at work. The Word of God definitely gives light for the path that God has given us. Our feelings of being misplaced dissolve, because in God we find our way.

We apply God's Word by putting into practice the Scriptures we have read. To apply means to express determination and purpose. We make up in our minds what we want to do. How many of us make New Year's resolutions to lose weight, read our Bibles more or spend more time with family? Some of these goals fall by the wayside; but those we focus on, write down, and develop plans for can be accomplished. We have the tools we need; we just need to be purposefully diligent. Life gives us practice. If we are struggling with following the crowd, we know 2 Corinthians 6:17 tells us to "come out from among them, and be ye separate." If we are being hindered by gossip, Ecclesiastes 5:2 says, "Be not rash with thy mouth."

How can we know how to respond to daily challenges if we never put God's Word into practice? If we don't apply God's principles to our lives, when challenges come we can only go on our own wits. God's Word helps us to distinguish between right and wrong. His Word helps us to see the dangers of bad choices before we jump in. We visualize the end before we indulge. It is good for us and helps us to be better. We begin to live prosperous spiritual lives.

"But be ye doers of the word, and not hearers only, deceiving your own selves" (James 1:22). When we just hear the Word and don't put it into practice, we deceive (err, go away from the truth) ourselves. There are tremendous spiritual blessings in following God's Word. We ask for wisdom (v. 5), and He generously gives—if we only ask.

Open Your Bible, Grab a Pen and Paper.

1. Are you choosy like Naaman or obedient like Noah?
2. Write down at least five benefits for following God.
3. Count the cost of those things you will have to give up to follow God. Beside each cost, list the level of difficulty (10 being the highest).
4. How much time are you willing to set aside for personal Bible study, prayer, and meditation?

5. What provisions do you need to make now to accomplish the benefits listed in #2?
6. How does your family feel about your decision to follow or not follow God? How does that make you feel?

 Application

At the end of the day, journal the challenges you faced and how you dealt with each.

Journal the areas of your life in which you feel strong and those in which you feel weak.

Memorize James 1:22.

Chapter 5
Cannot See For Looking

The old cliché, "The grass always looks greener on the other side" is what comes to mind when we cannot see for looking "or compare ourselves with some that commend themselves: but they measuring themselves by themselves, and comparing themselves among themselves, are not wise" (2 Corinthians 10:12).

We never learn who we can become if we are constantly looking and wanting the talents of others. Singles sometimes view the married lives of some in their church families and desire to be married. Married people may look at singles and desire to have their freedom. We may view sisters with talents for speaking and try to imitate their passion. A fellow church member may purchase a new house, and we ask God, "When will that happen for me?" The truth is, we may want to live in other people's shoes, but have we thought about what their lives may really be like? Does the married woman find enjoyment in her marriage? Is the single person really happy with her freedom? Do we want the responsibility of teaching women and being held accountable by God for what we present? Do we want the financial responsibilities of mortgages?

We can never learn who we can become if we are constantly looking and wanting the talents of others.

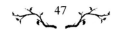

Driven By What We See

What drives us? Is the desire to have a husband, children, and a nice home our focus? Would a promotion on the corporate ladder put us in a blissful state? Would being admired and loved by everyone make us happy? Goals and dreams are necessary; God advocates us having goals. "Where there is no vision, the people perish: but he that keepeth the law, happy is he" (Proverbs 29:18). The desire to achieve and be the best we can be is great and should be supported. However, when we allow our desires to take precedence over our relationships with God; problems arise, and we cannot see for looking. It is perfectly okay to climb the corporate ladder; but if we are cheating and lying our way to the top, it becomes sinful. Do we elect to compromise the truth and forget our moral standards just to be accepted by the crowd?

We may begin to covet our possessions and not be willing to open our homes to share with others. Are our husbands and children our most prized possessions? Are we willing to let our children go and allow them to put into practice the biblical principles we've taught them? Would we do anything to present facades that our marriages are happy? Do we compromise the truth when we are asked where we attend worship? Satan (the enemy) is so happy when we turn our blessings into curses.

I'm reminded of when I first got married and how my husband's love continues to enhance my journey. We had been married for three to six months, and I had quietly allowed my Bible study time to grow less each day. During my single years, my Bible study was consistent on a daily basis. But I had become so caught up in this newly-chosen love that God was sitting on the back burner. Time progressed, and I put off my Bible study time for another day. I knew this did not please God. I fell on my knees during my devotional time and begged God for His forgiveness. I humbly asked God for His help to not allow His gift of marriage to become a curse. I did not want the love I had for my husband to be my first priority. I wanted our marriage to the best God could make it be. I knew that for this to happen, I had to seek

God first again. I explained this to my husband, and his support, as always, was encouraging. He understood the importance of my personal Bible study time. He welcomed and assisted me in having personal time with God.

In Luke 14, Jesus told the parable of the great supper. Many were called to attend this supper; the host announced that all things were ready, but the guests all began to make excuses.

The first said, "I have bought a piece of ground, and I must needs go and see it: I pray thee have me excused" (v. 18).

Another said, "I have bought five yoke of oxen, and I go to prove them: I pray thee have me excused" (v. 19).

Another said, "I have married a wife, and therefore I cannot come" (v. 20).

Jesus said, "If any man come to me, and hate not [love less] his father, and mother, and wife, and children, and brethren, and sisters, yea, and his own life also, he cannot be my disciple" (v. 26). We have to love less our fathers, mothers, spouses, children, brethren, sisters, and our own lives to truly be followers of God. Many will see that as harsh, but Christ did it! God wants to have first place, first priority and "preeminence" in our lives (Colossians 1:18). When we place God as the driver in our lives and allow Him to drive us toward a joyful and peaceful life, we realize the importance of Him taking the lead. Jeremiah 10:23 says, "O LORD, I know that the way of man is not in himself: it is not in man that walketh to direct his steps." When we attempt to steer our lives without God, we make bad choices.

God wants to have first place, first priority, and "preeminence" in our lives.

"Man that is born of a woman is of few days and full of trouble" (Job 14:1). When we are having difficulties seeking God first we should ask ourselves, "Why shouldn't I allow God to direct my steps? After all, He created me and wants the best for me."

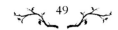

Caught Up in This Life

People used to say, "keeping up with the Jones," but now I think it's "keeping up with the Rockefellers." We are bombarded by TV shows that encourage being big spenders and purchasing large ticket items now. The media offers us so many options: magazine ads, TV commercials, billboards, newspapers, and the Internet. We must focus on the things we can't see, because those things are eternal. The things we do see are temporary (2 Corinthians 4:18).

The world places so much emphasis on the here and now. God tells us to focus on His Son's return and where we will spend eternity. "Lay not up for yourselves treasures upon earth, where moth and rust doth corrupt, and where thieves break through and steal: But lay up for yourselves treasures in heaven, where neither moth nor rust doth corrupt, and where thieves do not break through nor steal: For where your treasure is, there will your heart be also" (Matthew 6:19–21).

If we choose to trust in earthly riches, those things can rust and decay. Thieves can come into our homes and rob us. If we choose to store treasures in heaven, nothing or no one can destroy them. What we focus the majority of our time and energy on is where we are putting our treasures. If our goal is to be wealthy, we focus and find resources to achieve our goals. If our objective is to please God and do His will, then we seek His Word and obey it.

"For what is a man profited, if he shall gain the whole world, and lose his own soul? or what shall a man give in exchange for his soul?" (Matthew 16:26). We may get the accolades and commendations here on earth from others. We may be made to feel good about who we are and our earthly successes. But what benefit have we received if we are fearful to meet God in judgment?

The Scriptures instruct us not to trust in uncertain riches (1 Timothy 6:17). Proverbs 23:5 teaches that money will take wings and fly. We work long hours to make money, but the money is soon gone. "For the love of money is the root of all evil: which while some coveted after, they have erred from the faith, and pierced themselves through with many sorrows. But thou, O man of God flee these things; and follow after righteousness, godliness, faith, love, patience, meekness. Fight the good fight of faith, lay hold on eternal life, whereunto thou art also called, and hast professed a good profession before many witnesses" (1 Timothy 6:10-12).

Money is neither good nor bad. However, the love of money can lead us down a road of sorrow. Many people have left God to pursue riches. We must seek those things for which we don't have to write checks or give up our time with those we love. We must make a deliberate effort to guard our hearts (minds) and not chase after the cares of this world (Proverbs 4:23). We must stay focused on our goal of going to heaven and put off anything or any behavior that hinders us.

What Are We Focusing On?

What are we giving our attention to? Do we desire for our children to attend the best schools and go to Ivy League universities? Do we want them to do well in school and be godly examples to their peers? Do we want them to be teen missionaries or the most popular children in school? Do we want our families to be wealthy and live in the best neighborhoods? When we select mates, do we choose godly men or rich men? Do we live above our means and work constantly to provide our families the most popular material possessions? Would we prefer participating in company service projects rather than teaching someone how to become a Christian? What about attending Bible class on Sunday mornings? Have we sat down prayerfully and written out spiritual goals for our lives and for saving the lost? Have we prayed about these goals? Do they meet God's approval?

"If ye then be risen with Christ, seek those things which are above, where Christ sitteth on the right hand of God. Set your affection on things above, not on things on the earth. For ye are dead, and your life is hid with Christ in God. When Christ, who is our life, shall appear, then shall ye also appear with him in glory" (Colossians 3:1-4). If we have obeyed the gospel of Jesus Christ, then we must seek those things above (spiritual things that will help us grow closer to God). We set our desires on the things that are of God and not on the pleasures of this world. We are Christ's disciples, and He is our very life. If we have set our affections on things that are of God, then Jesus' return will be welcomed.

How Can I Change?

"[A]nd what hast thou that thou didst not receive? now if thou didst receive it, why dost thou glory, as if thou hadst not received it?" (1 Corinthians 4:7). We must realize everything that we have belongs to God. Job 1:21 says, "Naked came I out of my mother's womb, and naked shall I return thither: the LORD gave, and the LORD hath taken away; blessed be the name of the LORD."

In Luke 12:16–21, we read the parable of the rich fool: "The ground of a certain rich man brought forth plentifully: And he thought within himself, saying, What shall I do, because I have no room where to bestow my fruits? And he said, This will I do: I will pull down my barns, and build greater; and there will I bestow all my fruits and my goods. And I will say to my soul, Soul, thou hast much goods laid up for many years; take thine ease, eat, drink, and be merry. But God said unto him, Thou fool, this night thy soul shall be required of thee: then whose shall those things be, which thou hast provided? So is he that layeth up treasure for himself, and is not rich toward God." The rich man only thought of himself and trusted in his wealth. Our desire should be toward God and not toward obtaining wealth.

The rich man in Mark 10 asked, "Good master, what shall I do that I may inherit eternal life?" (v. 19). Jesus tells him not to commit adultery, kill, steal, bear false witness, cheat, and honor his father and mother. The rich man acknowledges obeying all of those commands from the time he was a boy. Jesus tells him to go and sell everything he owns and give it to the poor; then the man should come and follow Him (v. 21). The rich man "went away grieved" because he had an abundance of things (v. 22).

Jesus said, "Children, how hard is it for them that trust in riches to enter into the kingdom of God! It is easier for a camel to go through the eye of a needle, than for a rich man to enter into the kingdom of God" (vv. 24, 25).

Jesus' disciples asked, "Who then can be saved?" (v. 27).

Jesus answered, "With men it is impossible, but not with God: for with God all things are possible" (v. 27).

We learn in these passages that we cannot trust in uncertain riches and expect to reap the reward of eternal life. God is examining our hearts by watching what we do, how we live, and what we focus on. If we focus on God, whether we are rich or poor, then we are striving to obey God. Through His grace we are saved. God requires that we use our God-given resources, whether great or small, for His kingdom.

Open Your Bible, Grab a Pen and Paper.

1. Do you compare yourself with others?
2. What are your dreams and goals?
3. How do you plan to achieve them?
4. Do you have something or know someone that you value more than God?
5. In what area of your life do you make excuses?
6. Are you trapped by the materialism of this life? If so, why?
7. What can you learn from the rich man and the rich fool?

Application

Memorize Proverbs 23:5.

Memorize 1 Timothy 6:10–12 and Colossians 3:1–4.

Make a goal to give more to God financially.

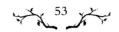

Chapter 6
I Must Be About My Father's Business

In Luke 2:49, we read of Jesus' focus: "I must be about my Father's business." Jesus came to earth to fulfill God's plan to save man through His death. "But He was wounded for our transgressions, he was bruised for our iniquities: the chastisement of our peace was upon him; and with his stripes we are healed" (Isaiah 53:5). Jesus denied His own desires to do what His Father had planned. Although criticized, lied about, mistreated, talked about, and spit upon, He stayed focused.

In Luke 4, we read of how Satan tempted Jesus. He had been in the wilderness 40 days and had eaten nothing (v. 2). Satan knew Jesus was hungry and demanded that He turn a stone into bread. Jesus said, "It is written, That man shall not live by bread alone, but by every word of God" (vv. 3, 4). Satan promises Jesus power and glory if He would bow down and worship him. Jesus responded, "Get thee behind me, Satan: for it is written, Thou shalt worship the Lord thy God, and him only shalt thou serve" (vv. 6-8). Satan then took Jesus to the high place of the temple and requested Him to jump off, realizing that God would send angels to aid Him (v. 9-11). Jesus answered, "It is said, Thou shalt not tempt the Lord thy God" (v. 12). The significance of Jesus being full of the Holy Spirit in verse 1 is the essence of why He was able to be victorious as Satan tempted Him. We need to make sure that we are daily spending time with God meditating on His Word. Jesus exhibits a humble spirit of submission and respect for His Father. He could have bought into acquiring fame and glory from man, but He knew what His purpose on earth was. Jesus had the power to do whatever He wanted, but He chose what was right. Jesus saw the end result when He was chosen to be the beginning. Sometimes we need to see ourselves going to heaven rather than the tasks before us. Christianity is like taking a test every day. In school, we prepare for tests by attending classes and studying. On test days if we have prepared, we generally receive passing scores.

In our Christian walk, we prepare by studying and putting into practice the things we have studied. Our tests come from living in a cruel and sinful world. We choose to follow evil or good. We resolve that just going to worship every time the doors open is not enough. A sincere, humble and submissive relationship with God will lead us on a path toward peace and transformation.

The Whole Duty of Man

"Let us hear the conclusion of the whole matter: Fear God, and keep his commandments: for this is the whole duty of man" (Ecclesiastes 12:13). The only way to make it through this life is to respect God and keep His commandments. This is man's purpose for being blessed to live on this time side of life.

"For even hereunto were ye called: because Christ also suffered for us, leaving us an example, that ye should follow his steps: Who did no sin, neither was guile found in his mouth" (1 Peter 2:21, 22). Christ suffered for us and left a beautiful example for us to follow. "Who gave himself for us, that he might redeem us from all iniquity, and purify unto himself a peculiar people, zealous of good works" (Titus 2:14). Jesus died for us, to free us from the evil of this world. His plan (once we surrender our lives to Him) is to help us desire to do good and be anxious for good works. One of His many gifts to help us accomplish this spiritual transformation is the gift of the Holy Spirit which we receive at the point of baptism (Acts 2:38).

God must see mothers seeking the Scriptures for wisdom to rear godly children. We need fathers that weigh their self-worth by God's

Word. We need children who are respectful and obedient to their parents. We need Christian families practicing *agape* love in their homes. We need families that are being strengthened by seeing God's Word put into action.

Be Still and Know

Psalm 46:10 instructs us to, "Be still, and know that I am God." We live in such a fast-paced society with no room to slow down. We can become so bombarded with busyness. One day we notice that our toddlers are now teenagers. Do we regret not having spent time playing Chutes and Ladders or staying the extra hour to jump on the trampoline? Do we long for more hours in the day to do the things that are worthwhile? For example: taking a walk in the park, visiting the sick and shut-ins, or encouraging someone. Living in such a fast-paced world is like riding a merry-go-round over and over with no time to stop and change seats. We have to make time to "stop and smell the roses." What are some of the things we need to stop and smell? Does going on a date with your husband sound nice? What about sitting down to dinner with every member of your immediate family? What about taking the time to read a full passage of Scripture without feeling rushed?

Satan loves it when we are so busy that we forget to be still and acknowledge God's creations. In our busyness, Satan finds our weak spots and challenges us with adversities. In our busyness, our guard is down. In our busyness, we don't realize the importance of sharing the gospel with a stranger on our ride in the elevator. In our busyness, we fail to see God's providential care. We take for granted arriving to work safely day after day. In our busyness, we fail to kiss our babies good-bye and forget to pray that they have a *In our busyness, Satan finds our weak spots and challenges us with adversities.* happy and safe day. In our busyness, we forget to greet our spouses with a hug or kiss before the work day begins.

Faith, Family, and Friends

We often hear the word *faith* and know it is something we should possess. "But without faith it is impossible to please him: for he that cometh to God must believe that he is, and that he is a rewarder of them that diligently seek him" (Hebrews 11:6).

Faith is believing in God and what He can do. If we don't believe in Him, we will not move toward serving Him through obedience. I'm reminded of Thomas, in John 20:24-29, when he saw Jesus after the crucifixion. The other eleven disciples had seen Jesus, and they began to tell Him, "[W]e have seen the LORD, But he said unto them, Except I shall see in his hands the print of nails, and put my finger into the print of the nails, and thrust my hand into his side, I will not believe" (v. 25). Jesus came to Thomas eight days later and said, "Peace be unto you" (v. 26). Jesus told Thomas to touch His hands and look for the nail prints. He then asked Thomas to put his hand into His side. He asked him not to doubt but to believe (v. 27). "Jesus saith unto him, Thomas, because thou hast seen me, thou hast believed: blessed are they that have not seen, and yet have believed" (v. 29). For those who believe, trust, and obey, many spiritual blessings await.

The family is the unit that God first put together (Genesis 1:27; 2:21, 22; 4:1, 2). It consisted of a man, woman and their offspring (Adam, Eve, Cain, and Abel). God wants the family unit to be a fortress of empowerment, learning about God and actively practicing discipline and acceptance. In the family unit we learn how to love and how to accept love. We learn how to forgive and be forgiven. We learn the sacredness of the marriage commitment. The principles of the Bible are taught and lived first by the parents. Children are taught about God, and as they mature they develop their own love for God.

Faith and strength in God is the foundation for the family. The family leader (the father) knows that Satan will attempt to strike his family unit. He makes sure that his family maintains its spiritual healthiness through observing, teaching and communicating. The father accepts his role as leader of the family and realizes that he answers first to

God (1 Corinthians 11:3). The family unit must be built upon a strong foundation so that when the storms of life come, the family will not be overtaken by Satan.

Luke 6:46–49 says,

> And why call ye me, Lord, Lord, and do not the things which I say? Whosoever cometh to me, and heareth my sayings, and doeth them, I will shew you to whom he is like: He is like a man which built an house, and digged deep, and laid the foundation on a rock: and when the flood arose [child on drugs or practicing promiscuity, unfaithful spouse, failing health, peer pressure], the stream beat vehemently [one trial after another] upon that house, and could not shake it [standing firm on the promises and compassion of God]: for it was founded upon a rock. But he that heareth, and doeth not, is like a man that without a foundation built an house upon the earth [our own wants and desires]; against which the stream did beat vehemently [child on drugs or practicing promiscuity, unfaithful spouse, failing health, peer pressure], and immediately it fell [exhibiting unforgiving spirit, pretending there is not a problem, focused on the negative, not believing God can or will help]; and the ruin of that house was great [children grow further astray, hatred and bitterness takes over, bring reproach upon the church].

We should be mindful of Psalm 127:1: "If it is not the LORD who builds a house, the builders are wasting their time. If it is not the LORD who watches over the city, the guards are wasting their time" (*ERV*). Our Christian homes and individual lives must be founded upon God's Word. If the family has prepared by growing spiritually, individually and collectively, it is able to weather the storms of life. We must arm our families with the Word of God and be dedicated toward our spiritual health. We must seek wisdom that will help us to expect the dangers that Satan uses to attempt to trap us. Walking by faith in God, we should choose the straight and narrow path (Matthew 7:14).

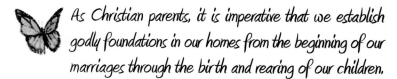 *As Christian parents, it is imperative that we establish godly foundations in our homes from the beginning of our marriages through the birth and rearing of our children.*

As Christian parents, it is imperative that we establish godly foundations in our homes from the beginning of our marriages through the birth and rearing of our children. Deuteronomy 6:5 commands that we love God with all of our heart, soul, and might. We are told first to plant the Word in our own hearts. We are to teach these principles diligently to our children and talk about God when we are sitting in our homes, as we go along our day, when we lie down, and when we rise up, (vv. 6, 7). The average person may consider such practices as fanatical, but God knows the importance of knowing Him. Our lives as parents, teachers, and professionals, whether good or bad, are "known and read of all men" (2 Corinthians 3:2). Upon my mother's passing, my earthly father was left with the responsibility to finish what she had started. I will always admire him for the way he took on the various roles of cook, mother, listener, and support. I'm sure there may have been times when he felt overwhelmed, but I always saw him doing what needed to be done. During my mother's illness, I remember the many times he would carry her to the car, because she was so weak and ill from the cancer. As we go through the cares and troubles of this life, let us use trying times to build upon our faith in God and strengthen our families. As parents, we must open the Word of God so that we can encourage and teach. We cannot afford to buy into the world's philosophy of what a marriage should be nor seek the world's guidelines in rearing our children.

If we open our ears to worldly views, others will tell us to never say "no" to our children. We will work two and three jobs to give our children everything their hearts desire. We will not discipline in love but allow them to disrespect us and themselves through bad behavior. We will try to live our lives through our children. We will encourage them to do all the secular things well and never encourage them to complete Bible assignments. We will seek to clean up their spills, so they never take ownership of their bad choices. We won't encourage our spouses to have alone time with God, so our families will not go astray. Wives will become dissatisfied and mentally abandon the family. We will live in fancy houses, but have nobody with whom to sit and eat dinner. These are all tools of Satan.

Opening our ears toward God will help us teach our children to earn rewards by good behavior. We will not live above our means, so we don't have to work two and three jobs. We will recognize that true peace and contentment comes from a relationship with God. We will discipline our children, so we can save their souls from the devil. We will use godly language so that our children know how to speak to us and others. We will be thankful and give God the glory when our children accomplish their goals. We will encourage participation in godly activities. We will encourage our children to select school activities that will not influence them to compromise their Christianity. We will continue to love and date our husbands so that our children experience firsthand examples of love. We should not uphold our children in their wrongdoing; they should learn consequences for their actions. We will seek God's Word more than any other reading material, so we stay dedicated to our families. We will make arrangements to always have dinner as a family, whether at home or in a restaurant. We will take the time to make our families "our" business.

I have heard people say, "I did all that, and my children still went astray!" "I was the devoted wife, and my spouse had an affair." I see this so often in the church. I can only say that God told us to sow the seed, be an example, and be prayerful that our children develop their own faith. To the married, I will only say that my husband will not have an affair as long as he is faithful to God. When either spouse stops being faithful to God, they are liable to do anything.

We should always be there for our spouses and our children. To be there is to listen attentively, to only pass righteous judgment, to use teachable moments to share God's teachings, and to live Christian lives before our spouses and children. I have often been told, "You cannot tell me anything about raising my children. You don't even have a teenager!" My answer is and will always be, "I don't have a teen yet, but I do remember being a teenager and the challenges that faced me. If I can impart some experience on what I learned and the wisdom my own mother gave to me, then it is beneficial to those that will listen."

We must make our families our ministries and have a willingness to practice unselfishness realizing that we are servants of God. We must have the desire to assist our families daily in drawing closer to God and help each family member learn his or her purpose for serving God. If we are personally making conscious efforts to know God, then we will pass our faith to our children. The greatest gift we can give our children is to know God. When this happens, we know they have developed their own faith. "When I call to remembrance the unfeigned faith that is in thee, which dwelt first in thy grandmother Lois, and in thy mother Eunice; and I am persuaded that in thee also" (2 Timothy 1:5). Paul was commending the faith of Timothy that he had seen by example from his mother and grandmother. Remember these wise words: "[E]very city or house divided against itself shall not stand" (Matthew 12:25).

Powerful Godly Friendships

Godly friendships are the essence of encouragement along this journey. I am reminded of the beautiful friendship between Ruth and Naomi. "And Ruth said, Intreat me not to leave thee, or to return from the following after thee: for whither thou goest, I will go; and where thou lodgest, I will lodge: Thy people shall be my people, and thy God my God" (Ruth 1:16). What a lovely, God-centered relationship! All Christian daughters-in-law should find joy in getting to know their mothers-in-law. I was personally blessed with my own Naomi. My husband's mother loved me as if I was her own daughter. She rejoiced in the love that I showered her son with. I thank God for knowing her as long as I did.

Genuine godly friendships glorify God. "Beloved, let us love one another: for love is of God; and every one that loveth is born of God, and knoweth God. He that loveth not knoweth not God; for God is love (1 John 4:7, 8). We show God to the world when we love one another. In Proverbs 18:24 we read, "A man that hath friends must shew himself friendly: and there is a friend that sticketh closer than a brother." The result of having friends is to be friendly. True friends are those that remember 1 Corinthians 13:4–7. They practice patience, show kindness, are not jealous, do not brag, are not prideful, are not rude or selfish, do not anger easily, and do not remember the wrong done in their friendship. How can a person practice these qualities? As we learn to love God and experience His love through our relationship with Him, these characteristics come through. Are we the type of friend that we would want to have?

"Faithful are the wounds of a friend; but the kisses of an enemy are deceitful" (Proverbs 27:6). Genuine friends will tell us the truth in love, considering themselves (Galatians 6:1), even though they may lose the friendship. "Am I therefore become your enemy, because I tell you the truth?" (Galatians 4:16). Their motive is pure. They will rejoice with us as we rejoice, and they will weep with us as we weep (Romans 12:15). What a blessing it is for Jesus to call us His friends if we do what He commands of us (John 15:14). Jesus is the greatest friend we could ever ask for. He is consistent and unwavering. Let us strive to take full advantage of this friendship. We would be wise to not invest in friendships with the world and realize that "evil communications corrupt good manners" (1 Corinthians 15:33). "Two are better than one; because they have a good reward for their labour. For if they fall, the one will lift up his fellow: but woe to him that is alone when he falleth; for he hath not another to help him up" (Ecclesiastes 4:9, 10). There is strength in numbers. Do we have godly friendships? We should strive to continue to be the type of friends that love others as God loves us.

Open Your Bible, Grab a Pen and Paper.

1. Why was Jesus dedicated to do God's will?
2. What does Ecclesiastes 12:13 mean to you?
3. What are some things that you can do to be still and know God?
4. What is your perception of a godly family? If you are single, what is your perception of a godly single person?
5. What are some ways you can encourage family and spouse time?
6. Do you have faith in God and His ability to save you?
7. How can you improve your faith?
8. What type of friend are you?
9. If you are a mother-in-law, how do you relate to your daughter-in law?

Application

Memorize Luke 2:49, Psalm 127:1, and Matthew 12:25.

Write what each of the above Scriptures means to you
and how you can apply them to your life.

Chapter 7
I Must Develop a Thankful Heart

What does it mean to be thankful? Is this an expression we only use at holidays and birthdays? How can we learn to be thankful to God? Do we express thankfulness during stormy weather? Do we express thankfulness for new cars? Do we show thankfulness for our old clunkers that still manage to get us to work? Do we give thanks for our food, health, families, and God's providential care?

Thankfulness: to feel or express gratitude. God desires that we develop thankful hearts. We know that when God asks us to do something, it is for our good.

Times of Want and Times of Prosperity

Paul said, "I am telling you this, but not because I need something. I have learned to be satisfied with what I have and with whatever happens. I know how to live when I am poor and when I have plenty. I have learned the secret of how to live through any kind of situation—when I have enough to eat or when I am hungry, when I have everything I need or when I have nothing" (Philippians 4:11, 12, *ERV*). Paul was able to understand how to be happy and thankful in times of prosperity and in times of want.

In Ecclesiastes 3:1 we are told: "To every thing there is a season, and a time to every purpose under the heaven." Many of us reading this book may be experiencing financial hardship, job loss, or depletion of savings due to an illness, or may be suffering from bad financial choices. Some of us may be enjoying the fruits of our labors, experiencing good health, or reaping the rewards of a good harvest.

God has promised us food, clothing, and shelter (our needs) as long as we are faithful to His Word (Matthew 6:30–33). We can rest with the assurance knowing that we will always have places to live and food to eat. I'm reminded of my friend, Sister Helen, and her example of accepting God's blessings. Sister Helen and I were roommates during my single years. I eventually married, and she did not want the responsibility of caring for her house because she was older. She applied for an apartment at one of our local senior towers, and soon she was offered living space. She sold her pretty little red brick house, as well as some pieces of furniture, and thankfully moved into the towers. She could've said, "I don't want to give up my house" or "I'd rather live in a nice condo." The lesson I learned was that she did not say either of those things. Her example of thankfulness for accepting what God had decided to give came from a humble heart. We become blinded when we see what we want rather than what God is willing to provide. God knew the future for Sister Helen, because a while later she became ill with cancer and needed to be at the Christian towers.

I often think of all the people and little children in the United States and foreign countries that go to bed hungry. They wake up with no breakfast to greet them. We take for granted always having something in the refrigerator to eat and drink. We throw away and waste food every day. I think of those parents barely making it financially and struggling to provide the basic necessities for their families. The blessing of being members of the Lord's body is that we will always be taken care of. Thank God for those who possess a willing and humble spirit to help those in their times of need.

Are You Abounding?

Abound: to multiply, to make over and above. Do you have more than you need? God holds us accountable for how we handle our possessions. Are we willing to share our finances with those who are unable to pay their light bills? Are we willing to purchase groceries for families even if they don't ask? Do we search within our church families to meet the phys-

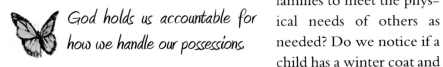 God holds us accountable for how we handle our possessions. ical needs of others as needed? Do we notice if a child has a winter coat and shoes to wear? Do we pray for God to open our eyes so that we can see the needs of others? Are we too busy buying for ourselves that we fail or put blinders on when we think of helping others?

Do we go in our closet and give our tattered possessions? I'm not saying we have to buy brand new items. However, I believe it is more of a self-sacrifice when we do. Allow me to give an example: If I'm saving to buy an expensive designer suit, and I see that a child does not have a coat and winter clothes, should I deny myself the new suit and take that money and purchase a coat and clothes for that child? I am a big advocate of hand-me-downs for children and adults. I have a five-year-old and am thankful for the sisters in our congregation who pass on their sons' clothes to mine. We must develop mindsets of thankful and selfless hearts. Satan will always put negative thoughts in our minds as we attempt good deeds. For example: "Why should I buy her children clothes? She has a job! I've bought her things before, and she did not wear them." "I don't want to offend anyone! My help could make them feel embarrassed." "Those people are not my responsibility; I have my own family to worry about!"

"But whoso hath this world's good, and seeth his brother have need, and shutteth up his bowels of compassion from him, how dwelleth the love of God in him? My little children, let us not love in word, neither in tongue; but in deed and in truth" (1 John 3:17, 18). We show our love for God by having compassion for others. Love is active, moving and driven to do something. "If a brother or sister be naked, and destitute of daily food, And one of you say unto them, Depart in peace, be ye warm and filled; notwithstanding ye give them not those things which are needful to the body; what doth it profit?"

(James 2:15, 16). We are admonished to "do good unto all men, especially unto them who are of the household of faith" (Galatians 6:10). "Beloved, let us love one another: for love is of God; and every one that loveth is born of God, and knoweth God. He that loveth not knoweth not God; for God is love" (1 John 4:7, 8). *Agape* love is doing what is in the best interest of others. God provides for our needs, not our wants. I'm reminded once again of Sister Helen and her act of unselfishness. She had managed to pay off her monthly furniture bill. Instead of buying herself something tangible, she made the choice to send that monthly bill amount to a faithful single sister battling cancer. She realized that her possessions belonged to God and sacrificially gave and lightened the financial load of another.

Are You Abased?

Abased: to make low, to be made low, humbled. God requires us to give and help based upon what we have. I have heard people say, "I would help, but I need help myself." I'm reminded of the lady who gave her two mites. "And Jesus sat over against the treasury, and beheld how the people cast money into the treasury: and many that were rich cast in much. And there came a certain poor widow, and she threw in two mites, which make a farthing [coins]. And he called unto him his disciples, and saith unto them, Verily I say unto you, That this poor widow hath cast more in, than all they which have cast into the treasury: For all they did cast in of their abundance; but she of her want did cast in all that she had, even all her living" (Mark 12:41–44). She was in need, but she gave what she could.

God requires us to give and help based on what we have.

God holds us responsible for what we have—whether a lot or little. God is fair. We may see someone in need of clothing and genuinely cannot assist. We could find out the cost of that item of clothing and have a certain number of members give us $5 to $10 each. We have met the needs of another person and allowed others to get involved; all participating receive a blessing. We may be unable to buy groceries for a family. However, we can invite them over for dinner. Jesus always did things for the good of others.

In the early church, the members sold their possessions to meet the needs (not wants) of others. Things were distributed based upon need (Acts 4:34, 35). Let us not be guilty of putting deaf ears toward the needs of others.

Guard Your Affairs With Discretion

We are advised to guard our affairs with discretion; this is the act of using wisdom. "A good man sheweth favour, and lendeth: he will guide his affairs with discretion" (Psalm 112:5). If a person is constantly asking for money, food, and a place to stay, it would behoove us to ask questions humbly considering ourselves. "But if any provide not for his own, and specially for those of his own house, he hath denied the faith, and is worse than an infidel [unbeliever]" (1 Timothy 5:8). "For even when we were with you, this we commanded you, that if any would not work, neither should he eat" (2 Thessalonians 3:10).

I am certainly not advocating helping those who are not trying to help themselves. As our elders would say, "Sometimes people need to hit rock bottom and lose some or all that they have so a lesson can be learned." This losing everything may mean that we hear the word *no* from friends and family. This may mean that the head of the household takes on an extra job. This may mean that we need to surrender to the reality of bad choices and living above our means. Job loss and health challenges can deplete money in savings. This is when the real test of true thankfulness is challenged. Are we still going to give to God during our losses? Are we only thankful when our pantries are filled to capacity? Do we find it difficult to be thankful when we are not sure of where our next meals are coming from? Are we thankful when we have $20 rather than $5,000? Do we question God's goodness when we cannot pay our gas bills, or do we swallow our pride and ask for help?

Thankfulness is a state of mind. It is being able to see the hope of eternity and the realization that what we see is temporary. We need to adopt the philosophy that when we get to heaven, paying the electric bill and having a place to stay is not going to matter. God has prepared a place for us (John 14:2, 3). In Matthew 6:25, 26, we are told not to worry about what we will eat, drink, or wear. God makes sure that birds have food to eat. We are worth more than the birds of the air. God has promised us the basic necessities as long as we are faithful.

What Motivates Us?

God judges our motives (the true intentions of what we do). First Corinthians 13:1, 3 encourages us to question our motives. We can do some really wonderful things for people; but if our actions are not motivated by love, what good are they? How many times have we spoken with people, and they have to tell us every good work they've done in detail? "Be careful! When you do something good, don't do it in front of others so that they will see you. If you do that, you will have no reward from your Father in heaven" (Matthew 6:1, *ERV*).

Do we get involved in church work to receive the praise of men? Mature, motivated Christians do not mind taking a back seat to praise. If they are praised by men, they give all the glory to God. I would rather my works be remembered by God and not man. When our motives are right we don't have to tell anyone, because we know that God sees and hears all things. We should always ask ourselves: "Why do I need this, or why am I doing that?" All we do should only be measured by God's Word. As we grow spiritually and accept God's Word, we will have the right mindset and be prayerful about keeping it.

In Luke 10, a lawyer asked Jesus, "Master, what shall I do to inherit eternal life?" (v. 25). The answer was, "Thou shalt love the Lord thy God with all thy heart, and with all thy soul, and with all thy strength, and with all thy mind; and thy neighbour as thyself" (v. 27). In verse

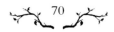

29, the lawyer asked Jesus, "And who is my neighbour?" Jesus then tells of the man who fell among thieves and was stripped of clothes and wounded. The robbers left him for dead. A priest came by, saw the hurt man and overlooked him (Luke 10: 31). A Levite looked at him and passed by as well (v. 32). A Samaritan came by and had compassion on the hurt man. He stopped what he was doing and bound up his wounds, pouring oil and wine over them. He sat him on his donkey and took him to an inn. While he was there, he took care of him (vv. 33, 34). The Samaritan left the next day, but he paid the innkeeper and asked that he take care of the hurt man. The Samaritan also said if additional money was needed for his care, he would repay the innkeeper when he came again (v. 35). The good Samaritan came out of his comfort zone and served a man in his time of need.

I'll Be Better When...

I have often heard the following phrases: "I'll have them over when I get a bigger house." "I'll serve and visit the sick when I get a better working vehicle." "Her house is so nice; mine just isn't good enough." "I just don't have enough room for another person." "I don't like having people over, their kids will mess up my well-kept home." "I just don't know about getting to know them; they are kind of strange."

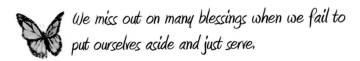 *We miss out on many blessings when we fail to put ourselves aside and just serve.*

Whatever happened to showing our thankfulness by sharing what God has given to us? Choosing not to have people over because we believe our houses are not what they should be is telling God we are unappreciative. We need to develop the mindset that if people are just coming to see what we have, we need to pray for them. If we feel this way for no reason, we need to pray for a thankful heart. We miss out on many blessings when we fail to put ourselves aside and just serve. Everything we have comes from God. We have nothing to brag or be haughty about. God created the air we breathe and allows us to breathe it. Job said, "Naked came I out of my mother's womb, and naked shall I return thither: The LORD gave, and the LORD hath taken away; blessed be the name of the LORD" (Job 1:21). Job lost everything, and he realized he had control over nothing. The things we have can be destroyed by fires, tornadoes, or thieves. We are forced then to adopt Paul's philosophy, "Not that I speak in respect of want: for I have learned in whatsoever state I am, therewith to be content" (Philippians 4:11).

"[G]odliness with contentment is great gain" (1 Timothy 6:6). Godliness is reverent (respectful) conduct. Contentment is a state of satisfaction. If our mindset is of God, then we have little trouble being content. We accept the things that God provides for us, and we use them to His glory. If we have cars, then we can provide transportation to those in need. If we have houses, we can invite people to eat, sleep, and fellowship with us. If we have money, we can help someone financially. If we are unable to help financially, we give up our time and schedule Bible classes or visit someone that is bereaved. We can babysit someone's child while he or she is being taught the Word of God. We should pray for ways to meet the needs of our congregation and put them into action. We have peace when we are showering others with blessings because of our thankfulness for what God has done in our lives.

Teach Me To Be Thankful

"Rejoice evermore. Pray without ceasing. In everything give thanks: for this is the will of God in Christ Jesus concerning you" (1 Thessalonians 5:16–18). Developing thankfulness is a mindset. It is the ability to recognize all the things, whether great or small, that God has done for us. We realize that all we have and are becoming is due to God's goodness and mercy. We should try keeping "thankful journals" and write down all the things that we are thankful for daily. We should meditate on and memorize Scriptures that encourage thankfulness. This helps us to acknowledge and repent when our thoughts are not grateful. Fellowshipping with godly people who are striving for the same thankful mindset encourages me to maintain a thankful heart. I pray to remember the times when I had not, so I can be thankful and humble when I have. We need to make a deliberate effort to always give thanks to God in our prayers before asking for anything.

The society we live in encourages the "all about me" syndrome. We rob ourselves of the spiritual blessing of contentment when we are competing with others to buy bigger and better. We allow Satan to flood our minds with the cares of the world because we are so focused on getting rather than giving. We become distracted by what we don't have rather than what we do have. When we learn our purpose for living, we will realize we have all we need.

The Christian family suffers when parents are focused more on buying designer things rather than the purchase of godly material. The Christian family also suffers when parents are too tired from working to read the Bible and pray with their children. It's all about rising above the temporaries that the world has to offer and realizing the need for the eternal.

Live in the Moment

All we have is the moment. Let us affirm to make this moment our very best by giving God our best.

By loving God our best.

By loving our family our best—just for today, with a hug and a smile.

By doing the important things—just for today, like giving thanks for our daily bread. Giving thanks for God waking us up from sleep.

By giving thanks to be among the living and showing the living how a life with Jesus can make our footsteps lighter and burdens easier to bear.

By honestly seeking God through prayer and making time to study His Word daily so that He can talk to us.

By sincerely trying to develop the mind of Christ so we can rest in the peace of His arms.

By listening without judging, by speaking as the oracles of God, and by meditating that we might not sin against Him.

By giving God all of our cares, so we can rest.

By praising His name through obedience.

By living the Christian life before others, and having a repentant and humble heart to make necessary changes, according to His divine Word.

We pray not to rob God of His opportunities to use us in these moments of life that He so richly bestows upon us.

We pray not to look in the past and become frustrated and bitter.

Help us, Lord, to just live faithfully in this moment.

Open Your Bible, Grab a Pen and Paper.

1. What is your definition of thankfulness?
2. Write down some times when you had plenty or when you needed more. How did you feel during those times?
3. If you've struggled financially, list the fears you had.
4. Do you find it difficult to help others?
5. Do you have compassion for others?
6. What motivates you to do things for others?
7. How did you feel after a good work was completed?

 Application

Memorize Ecclesiastes 2:1–22 and write down your thoughts.

Review Matthew 6:1–4 and write down your understanding of how to apply it to your life.

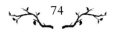

Section Three

The
Eye Opener

Chapter 8
Survival of the Faithful

Survival: **To continue to exist; to outlast**. Practicing true Christianity requires us to realize we are in a battle. We must wear the armor for battle and have the mindsets to win. In Ephesians 6:11, 14–17 we are told to "[p]ut on the whole armour [protection] of God, that ye may be able to stand against the wiles of the devil. ... Stand [be strong] therefore, having your loins girt about [belt on] with truth, and having on [your chest] the breastplate of righteousness [holy lifestyle]; And your feet shod [be ready] with the preparation of the gospel of peace [to tell of Jesus' death, burial and resurrection]; Above all, taking the shield of faith [your belief in God], wherewith ye shall be able to quench [capture the evil of Satan] all the fiery darts of the wicked. And take the helmet of salvation [a mind focused on heaven], and the sword of the Spirit, which is the word of God [Bible]."

I'm sure none of us would willingly leave the house without our clothes on. God wants us to wear all of our spiritual armor daily. We are not fully protected from Satan when we wear only portions of that armor. Once we realize that we are in a spiritual battle, we have to prepare for battle through knowing the Word of God. This battle is all about survival. It is not for the weak-minded, quitters, or the lazy. The battle is for those that are striving daily, repenting daily, studying daily, praying daily, and picking up those who have fallen. Jesus said, "But I have prayed for thee, that thy faith fail not: and when thou art converted, strengthen thy brethren" (Luke 22:32). How powerful and loving is that? Jesus is praying for us that our faith does not fail. Once we are convicted, we can influence others to be faithful. "Holding forth the word of life; that I may rejoice in the day of Christ [His coming], that I have not run in vain, neither laboured in vain" (Philippians 2:16). We have to do what we need to do in order to survive.

The race is not to the fastest, but the prize is for those that endure. "Know ye not that they which run in a race run all, but one receiveth the prize? So run, that ye may obtain" (1 Corinthians 9:24).

"Wherefore seeing we also are compassed about with so great a cloud of witnesses, let us lay aside every weight, and sin which doth so easily beset us, and let us run with patience the race that is set before us [perseverance], Looking unto Jesus the author and finisher of our faith; who for the joy that was set before him endured the cross, despising the shame, and is set down at the right hand of the throne of God" (Hebrews 12:1, 2).

For Those That Will

"For he that will love life, and see good days, let him refrain [stop] his tongue from evil, and his lips that they speak no guile [deceit, craftiness]: Let him eschew [to turn aside, avoid] evil, and do good; let him seek [search for] peace [a state of security and tranquility], and ensue [to pursue, follow after] it" (1 Peter 3:10, 11).

If we want to have good lives, we must not gossip and should be truthful. When we see evil we must run from it and search for the things that create peace. Gossip certainly produces division and strife. Many of us have said things that we would like to take back. We have been guilty of gossip and having the wrong motives in our speech. If we desire to survive, we must put away perverse speech. "Put away from thee a froward mouth, and perverse lips put far from thee" (Proverbs 4:24). "Out of the same mouth proceedeth blessing and cursing. My brethren, these things ought not so to be" (James 3:10).

How many of us have praised God and in the same breath spoken evil of our fellow sisters? We must always be mindful that God hears and sees all things. Would we say it if God was standing beside us? Think about it. He is! "Be not rash with thy mouth, and let not thine heart be hasty to utter any thing before God: For God is in heaven, and thou upon the earth: therefore let thy words be few" (Ecclesiastes 5:2).

"Casting down imaginations, and every high thing that exalteth itself against the knowledge of God, and bringing into captivity every thought to the obedience of Christ" (2 Corinthians 10:5). When we think evil thoughts, we need to capture those thoughts and repent immediately, so we don't act upon them. The Scriptures instruct us to be truthful. "Lie not one to another, seeing that ye have put off the old man with his deeds; and have put on the new man, which is renewed in knowledge after the image of him that created him" (Colossians 3:9, 10).

Swift to Hear and Slow to Speak

"Wherefore, my beloved brethren, let every man be swift to hear, slow to speak, slow to wrath: For the wrath of man worketh not the righteousness of God" (James 1:19, 20). We often practice the opposite and are quick to speak and slow to hear. We should offer words of encouragement and not words of despair. If I am speaking to someone whose daughter has just been sentenced to prison, and I say, "I'm so sorry. That is the worst thing that could happen to your daughter, and she is going to be even worse when she gets out! I'll pray for her and for you," how does that statement encourage the mother? When we don't know what to say, we need to be like Job's friends and just sit with that person silently.

If we go and visit someone ill with cancer, it certainly wouldn't be wise to talk about how our "Aunt Susie died of cancer a year ago." We should ask God to "Let the words of my mouth, and the meditation of my heart, be acceptable in thy sight, O LORD, my strength and my redeemer" (Psalms 19:14). Asking God this for each day He gives us will help us think before we speak.

Turning From Evil

Evil: iniquity, bad, malignant, useless, injurious. These words are all negative and certainly will not be of help to us as we attempt to survive. First Peter 3:11 instructs us to "eschew" evil (turn from it). The danger of following evil will turn malignant and eat at our very souls.

We search and find evil when we are practicing jealousy. We may seek friends that are unfaithful when we want to feel justified in our sinfulness. "Let them alone: they be blind leaders of the blind. And if the blind lead the blind, both shall fall into the ditch" (Matthew 15:14). "And he spake a parable unto them, Can the blind lead the blind? shall they not both fall into the ditch?" (Luke 6:39).

We may seek to sow discord when we have unforgiving spirits. "A false witness that speaketh lies, and he that soweth discord among brethren" (Proverbs 6:19). We may seek fornications or marriages when we believe that our biological clocks are running out. We may seek to ridicule others when we feel inadequate. We may seek to lie when we want to feel bigger. To turn from evil when we are jealous, we need to acknowledge it out loud, repent, and pray. When we desire the company of the wayward, we need to remember 1 Corinthians 15:33: "Be not deceived: evil communications corrupt good manners." When we deliberately sow discord, let us be mindful of Proverbs 6:16–19: "These six things doth the LORD hate: yea, seven are an abomination unto him: A proud look, a lying tongue, and hands that shed innocent blood, An heart that deviseth wicked imaginations, feet that be swift in running to mischief, A false witness that speaketh lies, and he that soweth discord among brethren." We should pray, "Keep back thy servant also from presumptuous [proud, rash, daring] sins; let them not have dominion over me: then shall I be upright, and I shall be innocent from the great transgression" (Psalm 19:13).

The only way we can get forgiveness from God is by forgiving others. "For if ye forgive men their trespasses, your Heavenly Father will also forgive you: But if ye forgive not men their trespasses, neither will your Father forgive your trespasses" (Matthew 6:14, 15). The hater never benefits from practicing hatred; he is eventually consumed by it. We need to ask God to fulfill us in our singleness, so we are not quick to commit fornication or marry outside of the Lord. "Can two walk together, except they be agreed?" (Amos 3:3). Second Corinthians 6:14 commands: "Do not be unequally yoked together with unbelievers: for what fellowship hath righteousness with unrighteousness? and what communion hath light with darkness?" If we are choosing to survive, we must be mindful that every ungodly behavior or thing with which we surround ourselves leads to our own fall.

In Pursuit of Goodness

Psalm 34:14 instructs us to "[d]epart from evil, and do good; seek peace, and pursue it." Good things are those things that are of God. The things of God are not normal to the fleshly man. We are to love our enemies. The flesh, however, says hate them, make sure they pay, let them know that we are angry with them. God says, "Therefore if thine enemy hunger, feed him; if he thirst, give him drink: For in so doing thou shalt heap coals of fire on his head. Be not overcome of evil, but overcome evil with good" (Romans 12:20, 21). This type of behavior goes against the natural man. It is easy to hold a grudge, but it takes effort, love, and humility to love your enemies.

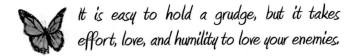

It is easy to hold a grudge, but it takes effort, love, and humility to love your enemies.

To pursue things that are good, we must seek God's Word to find those things. How can we measure goodness? Do we measure goodness by behavior? Do we call our children good by the way they conduct themselves? "And Jesus said unto him, Why callest thou me good? none is good, save one, that is, God" (Luke 18:19). The only one that is worthy to be called good is God. I'm not discouraging the offering of words of encouragement to our children or each othe, but.

God wants all of the glory and praise to be given to Him. We may have children that are obedient and have a 4.0 GPA, but their ability comes from God.

My 5-year-old son can recite information about characters in the Bible, and I quickly give him (what I call) a "smart boy hug." I ask, "Who made you so smart?"

He replies, "God did!"

I ask, "Who are you going to use it for?"

He says, "God!" Let us be mindful to teach our children and remind them where their talents and abilities come from. This breeds a heart of service and thankfulness for God's power. "But the fruit of the Spirit is love [the single attribute of God–John 3:16], joy [happiness, gladness, delight], peace [a state of calm security in God], longsuffering [to put up with another's weakness], gentleness [mildness], goodness [kindness], faith [steadfastness, trustworthiness], Meekness [quietness, gentleness], temperance [self-restraint]: against such there is no law [no limitation]" (Galatians 5:22, 23).

Everything we do must be based upon love. First Corinthians 13:1–7 teaches us to replace hatred with love. We move from sadness toward joy. We deliberately accept peace over despair. We put into practice longsuffering when we are met with words of discouragement. We practice gentleness as we teach others about Jesus. We show temperance to our supervisors as they hand us pink slips.

We make note of our weaknesses and ask God for help to change them into fruit of the Spirit. We know that we are growing spiritually when we can sincerely pray for our enemies. As our old habits rear their heads, we beat them back down with consistency. Jesus said, "Get thee hence, Satan: for it is written, Thou shalt worship the Lord thy God, and him only shalt thy serve" (Matthew 4:10).

Are We Too Big For Our Britches?

This phrase is often said to children by their parents. I can recall my mother saying it to me, and it was because I was being hardheaded. I'm

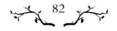

sure many of us know someone like this. These types of people in conversation are quick to give advice but never listen to their own words. If you climbed Mount Everest, so did they. If you skated in the Winter Olympics, they would tell you they did too. When they are admonished, they get angry. It does not matter if you spoke to them in meekness. This type of person always wants to do things his or her way. The path he or she chose is always far better than the one God would have him or her to be on. This type of person exhibits a rebellious spirit.

Rebel: **To resist authority, to revolt**. This type of spirit can never be of any purpose to God or anyone else. The Bible is a book of instruction and direction. How can we make changes in our lives if no one can tell us anything? "For rebellion is as the sin of witchcraft, and stubbornness is as iniquity and idolatry. Because thou hast rejected the word of the LORD" (1 Samuel 15:23).

"That this is a rebellious people, lying children, children that will not hear the law of the LORD" (Isaiah 30:9). A rebellious spirit results in bad choices that eventually grow to ache the bones. A person with this type of spirit enjoys seeing how far he or she can go without going over the edge. "Can a man take fire in his bosom, and his clothes not be burned? Can one go upon hot coals, and his feet not be burned?" (Proverbs 6:27, 28). We all know the answers to those questions. We cannot test the water and hope that we will come out unharmed. "No man can serve two masters: for either he will hate the one, and love the other" (Matthew 6:24).

The opposite of a rebellious spirit is a humble (lowly, meek) spirit. A non–rebellious person seeks to find answers through God's Word. He or she doesn't attempt to misquote Scripture for fulfillment of their desires. He or she is willing to receive help and direction from God's Word and people. Let us strive to put off a rebellious spirit, so we can truly reap the rewards of a humble spirit. "Humble yourselves there-fore under the mighty hand of God, that he may exalt you in due time" (1 Peter 5:6).

Developing Endurance

Endure: to abide, to bear up under suffering, to undergo, to sustain, putting up with, to tolerate. Endurance for the Christian is moving forward despite adversity. In Job 13:15, Job said: "Though he slay me, yet will I trust in him." I am so thankful for Job and what he went through. God has taken me on a personal journey toward spiritual transformation. I've learned to accept that He is the potter, and I am the clay (Isaiah 64:8). I continue to experience the battle of accepting change and choosing to follow God. This is my realization to obtain spiritual growth. I will never reach perfection, but I keep trying. As I repent Jesus' blood continually cleanses me. My battle will continue until I die or Jesus returns. That is why I desire to receive the "crown of life" (Revelation 2:10). I must be faithful unto death. This battle would not be worth fighting if we did not have eternal life to look forward to.

While on this journey we will experience challenges in our faith, like learning to forgive ourselves when we fall short and learning to forgive others when they hurt us. We continually learn to practice patience with others as we see how patient God is with us. We taste the beauty of humility in using our talents and the joy of giving God the praise and honor for our gifts. We take full responsibility for accepting the Word of God to grow from selfishness to selflessness.

We see our God-given talents in use through teaching and living the Word of God. We realize that as teachers of the Bible our judgment is double (James 3:1). Therefore, we take full responsibility for the things we teach and how we live our lives. We see the joy in young people's faces as we take time to let them into our lives. In doing this, we may suffer ridicule or be boycotted, belittled, and talked about. We realize that God is our only concern and the only one that we need to be striving to please. "Yea, and all that will live godly in Christ Jesus shall suffer persecution" (2 Timothy 3:12).

Eye View

It has often been said that we see what we are made of by the trials we go through. Trials cause us to question our faith. Troubles can make or break us. We grow closer to God or further away from God. Life is a road of changes, lessons, experiences, and growth spurts. "Knowing this, that the trying of your faith worketh patience" (James 1:3). Patience is a necessity when we choose to follow God. "Rejoicing in hope; patient in tribulation; continuing instant [steadfastly] in prayer" (Romans 12:12).

It has often been said that we see what we are made of by the trials we go through.

Once we decide to obey the gospel, we are promising to surrender our lives to God. We take up our cross and follow Him. We are also told to "let this mind be in you, which was also in Christ Jesus" (Philippians 2:5). We accept the fact that trials and tribulations are unavoidable. They will happen, and we must live expecting to receive them. We are so eager to accept God's goodness but not tribulation. "And we know that all things work together for good to them that love God, to them who are called according to His purpose" (Romans 8:28). Any situation that draws us closer to God should be welcomed. I am so thankful that Christ said before going to the cross: "O my Father, if it be possible, let this cup pass from me: nevertheless not as I will, but as thou wilt" (Matthew 26:39).

If life were great all the time, we would take it for granted and forget God. "Remove far from me vanity and lies: give me neither poverty nor riches; feed me with food convenient for me: Lest I be full, and deny thee, and say, Who is the LORD? or lest I be poor, and steal, and take the name of my God in vain" (Proverbs 30:8, 9). This Scripture reminds us to just be thankful for our daily bread and not to desire to be rich, because we may forget God. "But they that wait upon the LORD shall renew their strength [as we wait we grow spiritually]; they shall mount up with wings as eagles; they shall run, and not be weary; and they shall walk, and not faint" (Isaiah 40:31).

In our trials we make choices to either wallow in self-pity or take up our beds and walk. God helps us to stand in the face of doubt. He rewards us with blessings if we are suffering for doing what is right. We don't live in fear looking over our shoulders. "There is no fear in love; but perfect [mature] love casteth out fear: because fear hath torment. He that feareth is not made perfect in love" (1 John 4:18).

 We may not know what our futures hold, but we do know who holds the future.

Fear is the opposite of peace. We may not know what our futures hold, but we do know who holds the future. Negative thoughts during our trials come from Satan. He wants us to think that God is against us, and that we will never see light at the end of the tunnel. Spiritual growth comes when we pray for strength to endure—not for the pain to end. We will not get to that point overnight. However, as we go through life's challenges prayerfully, we are learning.

The Storms of Life

The storms of life may be our health failing or our children being unfaithful and disobedient. We may suffer marital problems or the loss of spouses or relatives. We may lose jobs and feel the effects of financial hardships. We may suffer ridicule from family and friends for serving God. We may battle with loneliness. We may experience the challenges of special-needs children.

My own personal health was challenged during my pregnancy. I was on home bed rest for more than a month and was later placed in the hospital for surgery. I spent three months of my pregnancy in a hospital bed. I could have been mad at God for not answering my prayer to have a good pregnancy. Instead, I used this as an opportunity to grow closer to God and be a positive example to my family members that came to visit as well as the nursing staff. I'm not saying I did not have bad days; but I had more good days than bad, because I was able to count my blessings daily. I filled my mind with the Word of God to combat my physical state. I was comforted by the power of God and the prayers of the righteous.

Breaking Through

The following are some steps I use while in a storm: (1) Keep your eyes on Jesus just as Peter did in Matthew 14:29–31: "And he said, Come. And when Peter was come down out of the ship, he walked on the water, to go to Jesus. But when he saw the wind boisterous, he was afraid; and beginning to sink, he cried, saying, Lord, save me. And immediately Jesus stretched forth his hand, and caught him, and said unto him, O thou of little faith, wherefore didst thou doubt?" As long as Peter's eyes were on Jesus, he did not sink; but as soon as he took his eyes off Jesus, he began to sink. This is what happens to us. We start to sink in self-pity and despair when we stop focusing on the power of God. We must learn to view life's challenges from God's perspective. (2) Assess the problem. Can you improve the situation? If you can, then go for it. If you cannot, pray for strength to endure and for God to reveal what He wants you to learn. (3) Keep serving God, keep teaching, visiting the sick, and sending cards to the weary. This will help you to stay focused and not have a pity party. (4) Make a list of all the things you are thankful for. Write down how you are doing and honestly feel daily. Seek to locate Scriptures that will aid in changing your negative thinking. (5) Talk to a faithful and honest Christian who loves you sincerely. Make sure this person can be spoken to confidentially. (6) See yourself in the battle using the fruit of the spirit for combat. (7) After you get through it, go and tell someone so you can help them to endure. "And let us not be weary in well doing: for in due season we shall reap, if we faint not" (Galatians 6:9).

Open Your Bible, Grab a Pen and Paper.

1. What is hindering you from surviving spiritually?
2. Read and explain Ephesians 6:11, 14–17.
3. What is the most difficult challenge in your quest for spiritual growth?
4. Are you quick to hear and slow to speak? If not, how can you work on that?
5. Do you have a humble or rebellious spirit? Why or why not?
6. Do you find yourself cleaving to things that are good or evil?
7. How can you develop endurance during trials?
8. How can you use your trials to encourage others?

 Application

Memorize Isaiah 40:31 and Galatians 6:9.

Keep a "thankful journal" for reflection and growth.

Chapter 9
We Are Just Passing Through

D o you have any friends or relatives that are in the military? The military lifestyle is often one of constant movement. Your feet are never truly planted in one spot for a long time. The benefit of this lifestyle is being able to see the world and meet new people. As Christians, we must accept that we are just passing through life. We are preparing for our final destination.

This Is Not My Home

This life is temporary; we were not created to stay here forever. Our lives are a practicing ground for heaven. The world's present state is one of chaos, confusion, crime, selfishness, and fear. Why would we want to stay here? God offers us hope, peacefulness, and joy in the midst of a turbulent and unruly society. We create the desire to stay when we wrap ourselves in the clothing of the world. If we seek to please man more than God, we have a desire to stay. If we have more worldly friends than Christian friends, we desire to stay. If we always manage to make time to volunteer in the community and never offer to teach Bible classes, then our desire to stay here is more important. If our career achievements have greater value than our desire to be faithful to God, we want to stay here.

Not Meant to Stay

"[I]t is appointed unto men once to die, but after this the judgment" (Hebrews 9:27). If we are blessed to stay here for a while, we become old. Our teeth aren't like they used to be, and we have a few more aches and pains. We may be ready to retire, and our hair may be turning gray. This is called the aging process; we will all experience it. Some of us may die young, and some may die old. Death is not something that the majority of us like to talk about. We will plan our retirements and establish financial goals, but we may fail to plan for where we will spend eternity. As young people, we may see ourselves living for a long time. I experienced death firsthand when I lost my mother to cancer at the age of 13. Four years later, my older brother died from leukemia. We cannot run from death nor pretend that it will not happen—regardless of our age.

We must always ask ourselves: If Jesus came back today, would we be ready to see Him? Would we be fearful to see His face? If we were flying on a plane and it crashed, what would our thoughts be? Are we living with the expectation of dying? I'm not saying that we walk around morbid and hopeless. Jesus could have had that mindset, but He did not. He knew that He was going to endure a cruel and inhuman death on the cross, yet He stayed focused and understood what His life on earth was to accomplish. Are we living our lives to serve ourselves or others? Will our past and recent decisions hinder us from seeing God's face in peace? Will our names be "written in heaven" (Luke 10:20)? Heaven will be a place of rest (Hebrews 4:9–11). There will be no more tears or pain (Revelation 21:1–4). It is a house "not made with hands" (2 Corinthians 5:1). We will "ever be with the Lord" (1 Thessalonians 4:17).

On the other hand, hell is a place of torment and pain (Revelation 14:11). It is a place of "everlasting fire" (Matthew 18:8). The devil and his angels will be there (25:41). All unbelievers and liars will have their place there (Revelation 21:8), as well as the disobedient (Romans 2:8, 9). The punishment there is everlasting (2 Thessalonians 1:8, 9).

Do we serve God out of fear? Many of us do in the beginning. However, as we grow in our allegiance to God, we serve out of gratitude and humility. "If ye love me, keep my commandments" (John

14:15). We have access to Jesus' blood as we repent; His blood cleanses us (Hebrews 9:22). We cannot work our way into heaven; however, works play a part in our faithfulness toward God (James 2:17).

We must be found putting forth the effort, and Jesus' blood is the cleanser toward salvation. We should never give up or faint (Galatians 6:9). The race is not for the first person who crosses the finish line but for those who endure. (Matthew 24:13; Mark 13:13).

"For that ye ought to say, If the Lord will, we shall live, and do this, or that" (James 4:15). Do we really believe that God is in control? Adopting the concept that we are not here to stay is acknowledging that Christ is coming back. Judgment will begin in the house of God (1 Peter 4:17).

Adopting the concept that we are not here to stay is acknowledging that Christ is coming back.

Paul was caught betwixt whether to depart or stay (Philippians 1:21–23). If we have the mindset of Paul, to stay should be to help God's people for the furtherance of the gospel. If we desire to leave, it should be because we are ready to be with Him. Jesus said that He has prepared a place for us (John 14:2). We have a home "not made with hands, eternal in the heavens" (2 Corinthians 5:1).

If This Was Our Last Day

We ought to live each day as if it was our last. All we have is right now, and that is a gift from God. "For what is your life? It is even a vapour, that appeareth for a little time, and then vanisheth away" (James 4:14). Have we spent our days in devotion to God? Did we share the gospel with someone today? Did we stop and thank God for waking us up? Did we make time to pray with our children? Did we tell our spouses that we love them? Let us be ever mindful of the legacy that we are leaving. What really matters is where we will spend eternity.

We are the salt of the earth (Matthew 5:13). Our lives must be used for something. We are the light of the world (vv. 14–16); with so much darkness (evil), we need to be planting seeds for the discouraged and fainthearted to see God. If we are living as God instructed, we will give "light unto all that are in the house" (v. 15). We help others to find their way through God's Word. A godly lifestyle glorifies God and gives hope to the misdirected.

Open Your Bible, Grab a Pen and Paper,

1. Recall a moment when you lost someone close to you. How did you handle it?
2. Do you want to go to heaven? Do you believe heaven exists?
3. Do you believe we are not here to stay? If so, why?
4. Do you desire to stay or leave? Why?
5. How do you feel about the aging process?
6. Are you being the salt of the earth?
7. How do you want to be remembered?

Application

Write down your spiritual goals and a plan of action to accomplish them.

How can you live each day as if it were your last?

Memorize James 2:17; 4:14.

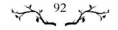

Chapter 10
Awake Thou That Sleepest

Asleep: **In a state of sleep, the lack of sensation, numb, not alert**. Many of us are fast asleep as we walk along our Christian journey. "Wherefore he saith, Awake thou that sleepest, and arise from the dead, and Christ shall give thee light. See then that you walk circumspectly, not as fools, but as wise, Redeeming the time, because the days are evil. Wherefore be ye not unwise, but understanding what the will of the Lord is" (Ephesians 5:14–17). We are commanded to awake and walk circumspectly (being aware of our surroundings) redeeming the time (to use time wisely) because we are living in dangerous times. Do not be unwise; seek God's Word to find out what the will of God is. "Therefore let us not sleep, as do others; but let us watch and be sober [calm, temperate, sound minded]" (1 Thessalonians 5:6).

Are You Asleep or Awake?
Do you go through your day unaware of your surroundings? Do you begin your day in a rush? Do you get the kids dressed in a hurry? Are you constantly late for worship? Is breakfast just a glass of juice? Is your entire day spent unorganized?

First Corinthians 14:40 tells us: "Let all things be done decently and in order." We need to plan our days in advance. We don't live for tomorrow. It is wise to prepare, but we should bear in mind "if it is God's will." Life will sometimes have those unexpected moments, especially if we have infants and toddlers. Our Sunday mornings can be spent taking time to eat breakfast as a family. We can have small devotionals to prepare our minds for worship to God. Clothing selection can be done the night before. I personally find that my mind is not frazzled before service if I take the time to meditate alone in the morning or with my husband. We are commanded to worship "in spirit and in truth" (John 4:24).

One of the areas that may be lacking is making a conscious effort to prepare for Sunday morning worship. We think more clearly when we've had time to think about God before we begin our day. "Wherefore lay apart all filthiness and superfluity of naughtiness, and receive with meekness the engrafted word, which is able to save your souls" (James 1:21).

My heart goes out to all those young Christian mothers with small babies and toddlers. I was on time for every service until I had our son. I work hard at doing my best and to be my best. I know that God understands and embraces us as we anxiously get our children ready for service.

Do we sleepwalk as mothers? Do we guide our houses? Do we allow our children to hang out with negative influences? Do we encourage them? Do we leave no room for failure? Do we seek to assist in improving their shortcomings? Do we discipline in love or in anger? Are we jealous of their successes?

I love the story of Hannah and her desire to have a baby (1 Samuel 1:1-27, 2:11). She promised to give her son back to God if she was blessed to have a child. God answered her prayer, and she kept her promise. Samuel later became a humble and committed servant of God. Are we preparing to give our children back to God? Do we have Bible study and prayer with them daily? Do they see us studying and praying? Do we make time to teach them about God? Are we praying that through our teaching they develop their own faith?

Characteristics of a Rare Jewel

Often, we refer to Proverbs 31 and the virtuous woman but leave out her son, King Lemuel. It is noted at the beginning of that chapter that King Lemuel is sharing with us the characteristics of a virtuous woman that his mother taught him (v. 1). We need to share this chapter with our sons for characteristics to look for in a potential mate.

The characteristics of the virtuous woman are certainly attributes that we can put into action today. We can also encourage our daughters to follow in her footsteps. She is virtuous (chaste, pure) and more valuable than jewels (Proverbs 31:10). The world encourages promiscuity and the freedom to express yourself sexually. "The heart of her husband doth safely trust in her" (v. 11). Can my husband trust me? When he shares a private matter about himself, am I eager to tell others or do I pray for him? Do I belittle him, or am I his biggest supporter? Will I "do him good and not evil all the days of my life" (v. 12)? Am I there for him? Do I respect my husband by allowing him to be the head of the household? Do I undermine him and question his actions? Am I seeking his best interests? Do I shower him with words of truth, so he is confident about my love for him? Am I affectionate toward him?

She "[w]orketh willingly with her hands. ... She looketh well to the ways of her household, and eateth not the bread of idleness" (vv. 13, 27). If we are blessed to not work outside our homes, do we seek to raise our children to be godly? Do we keep clean and neat homes? Do we prepare dinners for our families or waste money by eating out constantly? Do we willingly accept our roles as wives and mothers? Do we put forth the same efforts although we work outside of the home? "She girdeth her loins with strength" (v. 17). Are we mindful to take care of ourselves physically? Do we seek to do godly things with other faithful women so that we are renewed spiritually?

"Her children arise up, and call her blessed; her husband also, and he praiseth her" (Proverbs 31:28). Do we practice *agape* love (doing what is in their best interest) toward our children? Are we careful not to show favoritism among our children? As he greets you after a long day, are you the type of wife with whom your husband would rejoice? "Favour is deceitful, and beauty is vain: but a woman that feareth the LORD, she shall be praised" (v. 30). Are we mindful to feed our spiritual bodies, so we can teach by example? Are we more concerned about our physical beauty than our inner, spiritual beauty?

The Christian race is not for those who enjoy sleeping; it is for those who are alert and want to get better. The race is for the strong and not the weak-minded. We gain strength by reading God's Word. We adopt stamina by remembering all the things that God has brought us through. We develop desire for our Father *The Christian race is not for those who enjoy sleeping; it is for those who are alert and want to get better.* by constantly giving thanks and recognizing all that He has done.

"Except the LORD build the house" (Psalm 127:1). We must build our homes upon the Word of God, so we as families can fight against Satan and his devices. "Let your loins be girded about, and your lights burning; ... Blessed are those servants, whom the lord when he cometh shall find watching: ... Be ye therefore ready also: For the Son of man cometh at an hour when ye think not" (Luke 12:35, 37, 40).

> And why call ye me, Lord, Lord, and do not the things which I say? Whosoever cometh to me, and heareth my sayings, and doeth them, I will shew you to whom he is like: He is like a man which built an house, and digged deep, and laid the foundation on a rock: and when the flood arose, the stream beat vehemently upon that house, and could not shake it: for it was founded upon a rock. But he that heareth, and doeth not, is like a man that without a foundation built an house upon the earth; against which the stream did beat vehemently, and immediately it fell; and the ruin of that house was great (Luke 6:46–49).

Therefore, my beloved brethren, be ye steadfast, unmoveable, always abounding in the work of the Lord, forasmuch as ye know that your labour is not in vain in the Lord (1 Corinthians 15:58).

Open Your Bible, Grab a Pen and Paper.

1. Would you consider yourself asleep or awake spiritually?
2. How can you practice walking circumspectly?
3. Because there is always room for improvement, how could you make better use of your time?
4. What does it mean to "watch and be sober"?
5. If you find yourself in a rush, how can you prepare for your day to run smoothly?
6. How can you prepare to give God your best?
7. What characteristics of the "virtuous woman" would you like to develop?
8. How can you build a strong Christian home?

Application

Memorize Luke 6:46–49.

Practice the "golden rule." Treat others the way you want to be treated (Matthew 7:12; Luke 6:31).

Write down the names of those persons to whom you desire to be kinder and put a plan into action.

Section Four

The Cleanser

Chapter 11
The Goodness of God

K nowing that the goodness of God leadeth thee to repentance" (Romans 2:4). I have often heard gospel preachers use the alphabet to describe God, so I came up with my own version: **A** is for Alpha, because He is my beginning (Genesis 1:1). **B** is for bold; through our faith, we may approach God with boldness and confidence (Ephesians 3:12). **C** is for Christ; God sent His Son to die for me (Romans 5:6). **D** is for dedicated; God cares for my well–being (2 Peter 3:9). **E** is because His name is excellent (Psalm 148:13). **F** is because He is my Father (2 Corinthians 6:18). **G** is because He's so good to me (Psalm 85:12). **H** is for honest; God cannot lie (Titus 1:2). **I** is intelligent. God is the creator of all; no one else could do all that He's done (Genesis 1). **J** is for joy; we should be joyful that we belong to Him (Psalm 66:1). **K** is for king; we should give honor and glory to Him (1 Timothy 1:17). **L** is for love; "God is love" (1 John 4:8). **M** is for merciful. God is merciful and gracious (Exodus 34:6). **N** is because I need Him in my life (Jeremiah 10:23). **O** is for omnipotent, He is almighty and all–powerful (Revelation 19:6). **P** is for patience; God is patient with me (Psalm 40:1). **Q** is for quick, because His Word is quick and powerful (Heb 4:12). **R** is for reverent; "[H]oly and reverent is his name" (Psalm 111:9). **S** is for safety; I am safe in His arms (1 Peter 5:7). **T** is for teaching; God is constantly teaching and guiding me through His Word (Proverbs 16:9). **U** is for upright; "good and upright is the Lord" (Psalm 25:8). **V** is for victorious; He makes the victory possible through His Son, Jesus (1 Corinthians 15:57). **W** is for wise; He is "the only wise God," and we should honor Him (1 Timothy 1:17). **X** is for x–ray, He can see through me (Psalm 94:11). **Y** is because God yearns for all to "come to repentance" (2 Peter 3:9). **Z** is for my zealousness to follow God (Psalm 119:59, 60).

God is

> The LORD is my light and my salvation; whom shall I fear? the LORD is the strength of my life; of whom shall I be afraid? … One thing have I desired of the LORD, that will I seek after; that I may dwell in the house of the LORD all the days of my life, to behold the beauty of the LORD, and to enquire in his temple. … I had fainted, unless I had believed to see the goodness of the LORD in the land of the living. Wait on the LORD: be of good courage, and he shall strengthen thine heart: wait, I say, on the LORD (Psalm 27:1, 4, 13, 14).

I'm sure many of us have awakened during the night in total darkness and in our attempt to get up, have begun to stumble. There is no stumbling to find our way when we acknowledge God as the light we need to direct us on our journey.

Salvation (deliverance, saved, rescued, having forgiveness of sins) is made possible through the blood of Jesus. We have absolutely nothing to fear when we know that God is there. He so richly gives us strength to run this race called life. When we learn to depend only upon God, we become less and less afraid. Our first desire must be to go to heaven, so we can witness His presence firsthand. God's providential care (provisions, safety) for His children is indescribable. Through our learning of Him, we gain patience, tenacity, and strength.

God is so powerful and wise. In Exodus 14:21–30, the children of Israel needed to escape from Pharaoh's army, and God gave Moses the power to part the sea. God caused manna (food) to rain from heaven (16:4, 35). God brought plagues (water to blood, frogs, lice, flies, dis-

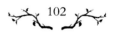

ease of farm animals, boils, hail, locusts, darkness, and death of the firstborn children and animals) against Pharaoh, because of his refusal to let the children of Israel go. All the Egyptians suffered because of Pharaoh's disobedience (7:20, 21; 8:2-6, 16, 17, 24; 9:3-6, 8-11, 22-25; 10:12-15, 21-23; 12:29, 30).

God protected Shadrach, Meshach, and Abednego from the intensity of a fiery furnace (Daniel 3:15-27). God caused Nebuchadnezzar to wander in the wilderness and become as an animal because of his failure to acknowledge Him (4:33). When Daniel was in the lions' den, God sent an angel to shut the mouths of lions because of Daniel's faithfulness to him (6:15-23). We see God's desire for us to respect Him. We see His reward to those who are faithful and His desire to influence the unbeliever. Through God's power, Naaman was cured of his leprosy by washing in the Jordan River (2 Kings 5:1, 9-14). We see God's request for us to follow only His direction so that we can reap the benefit of obedience.

His Divine Plan

In Isaiah 53:1-12, we read of the plan that God already had in place to save man through His Son, Jesus. "Yet it pleased the LORD to bruise him; he hath put him to grief: when thou shalt make his soul an offering for sin, he shall see his seed, he shall prolong his days, and the pleasure of the LORD shall prosper in his hand" (v. 10).

God created the world and made man. He took a rib from Adam and made woman. Adam was advised to take care of the Garden of Eden. God gave Adam specific instructions not to eat from the tree of the knowledge of good and evil (Genesis 1:1, 27; 2:17, 22). Eve was tempted by Satan and wanted to be wise. She and Adam ate fruit from the forbidden tree (3:2-6). Suddenly, they were exposed and knew that they were naked. Sin entered into the world. They sewed fig leaves together and made them as aprons to cover themselves (v. 7). They heard the voice of God and tried to hide among the trees (v. 8). God called Adam's name, "Where art thou?" (v. 9). But God knew where he was. Adam said that he had heard God's voice and was afraid. He hid himself because he was naked (v. 10). God asked Adam how he knew that he was naked and asked if Adam had eaten from the tree that He told him not to eat from. Adam's response was to blame Eve because she had given him the fruit (vv. 11, 12). Eve quickly blamed Satan (v. 13). They were both cursed by God and driven out of the Garden of Eden.

God's plan of salvation is to hear (Romans 10:17); believe (Hebrews 11:6); repent (Luke 13:3); confess (Romans 10:10); and be baptized (Acts 2:38). All of these steps must take place in order for us to be added to the body, the Lord's church (v. 47).

Shall We Continue

"What shall we say then? Shall we continue in sin, that grace may abound? God forbid. How shall we, that are dead to sin, live any longer therein?" (Romans 6:1, 2). Once we obey the gospel, our old sins are passed away (forgiven). However, our sinful habits do not go away; we may still desire to do wrong. The key is to overcome by replacing old habits with godly habits. For example: If we were liars, we practice truthfulness. The difference is not to habitually commit sin; now we make a conscious effort to do what is right. Once we learn better, we do better.

I have heard gospel preachers often say, "Sin will take you places you never thought you would go, and will keep you longer than you meant to stay." We are in the flesh (human nature, the sensuous nature of man). However, God made us free moral agents. We have the option to choose good or evil. God could have made us like robots, but He did not.

We will choose to do good if we have inclined our ears to hear and our hearts (minds) to apply His Word. We choose evil if we have not inclined our ears to study and meditate on His Word. "For as a man thinketh in his heart, so is he" (Proverbs 23:7). Whatever we think we are is what we become. Jesus said, "But those things which proceed out of the mouth come forth from the heart; and they defile [pollute, make profane, unclean, corrupt] the man. For out of the heart proceed

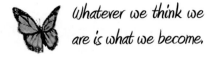

Whatever we think we are is what we become.

evil thoughts, murders, adulteries, fornications, thefts, false witness, blasphemies: These are the things which defile a man" (Matthew 15:18–20). That is why it is vitally important that we heed Proverbs 4:23: "Keep thy heart with all diligence; for out of it are the issues of life." We must realize the importance of guarding our hearts and being mindful of what we think on, view, read, and consider those with whom we associate. "Stand in awe, and sin not: commune with your own heart upon your bed, and be still" (Psalm 4:4). "[W]hen I would do good, evil is present with me" (Romans 7:21). Even when we have prepared ourselves, we find that we still sin. We know the right thing to do, but sometimes we elect not to do it. We need to develop the mindset to sin less.

There are three ways that Satan tempts us: lust of the flesh (1 Peter 2:11), lust of the eyes (Genesis 3:6) and the pride of life (James 4:6, 7; 1 John 2:16). The lust of the flesh consists of those things we desire that can take precedence over God. Those things war against the soul (1 Peter 2:11). The lust of the eyes is what we see. Eve saw that the fruit on the tree of the knowledge of good and evil could make her wise (so she thought). We may see the cars we want to drive and the houses we want to live in or other women's husbands we want to have. The pride of life is a proud look. We know everything, and no one can tell us anything. This is a rebellious spirit. We are drawn away and enticed by our own desires and weaknesses (James 1:14). Satan tempts us in areas that we are unaware of as well as those areas in which we are weak.

God does not tempt us. "Let no man say when he is tempted, I am tempted of God: For God cannot be tempted with evil, neither tempteth he any man" (v. 13). He does not want our belief system about sin to cause us to become as hypocrites; placing degree levels on sin like the Pharisees. "Woe unto you, scribes and Pharisees, hypocrites! for ye are like unto whited sepulchres, which indeed appear beautiful outward, but are within full of dead men's bones, and of all uncleaness" (Matthew 23:27).

We fool ourselves when we think that adultery is far worse than a lie. God looks at sin on all the same levels. Lying or having pride (Proverbs 6:17) is just as bad as committing adultery or stealing. "For all have sinned, and come short of the glory of God" (Romans 3:23). "If we say that we have not sinned, we make him a liar, and his word is not in us" (1 John 1:10). "Therefore to him that knoweth to do good, and doeth it not, to him it is sin" (James 4:17). We cannot forget our responsibility to put forth the effort to do what God says. No person on earth is perfect and sinless. When we develop this type of thinking we lose our influence to save the lost. People that are lost do not come into the church having lived perfect lives. If this was the case, none of us would need Jesus or the church. Our testimony to people is to humbly tell them about our shortcomings and struggles. Jesus said, "He that is without sin among you, let him first cast a stone" (John 8:7).

When we share our weaknesses with others, walls are torn down and people feel free to question their sinful mindsets. They see the power of God being used to change us from alcoholics to evangelists. We go from fornicators to those that practice abstinence. We move from lying toward being truthful. We acknowledge our transformation as God's power and take no credit for our spiritual transformation thus far.

One may say, "Well if I'm in the flesh and I'm going to mess up anyway, why should I try?" God requires us to make a choice, just as Joshua did in Joshua 24:15: "And if it seem evil unto you to serve the LORD, choose you this day whom ye will serve; whether the gods which your fathers served that were on the other side of the flood, or the gods of the Amorites, in whose land ye dwell: but as for me and my house, we will serve the LORD." Daily we make a choice of whom we will serve.

Jesus prayed to God in the garden before His crucifixion, but He did the will of His Father (Matthew 26:39, Mark 14:36). "Those things, which ye have both learned, and received, and heard, and seen in me, do: and the God of peace shall be with you" (Philippians 4:9).

Satan is the god of this world. Therefore, all types of evil exist. "Love not the world, neither the things that are in the world. If any man love the world, the love of the Father is not in him" (1 John 2:15). To obey and follow God is far better than any sin.

The temporary pleasures we get from sin are just that—temporary. The opportunity by God's grace to live a peaceable and joy-filled life is a treasure to be valued and shared with all who will hear. The treasure is not that we don't have problems; rather, it's the ability to accept God's Word and apply it to our problems. We trust and rest in the assurance of God's power.

God is an advocate for a sincere heart and for those who sincerely try to do His will. Many refer to Hebrews 11 as the "hall of faith." "Wherefore seeing we also are compassed about with so great a cloud of witnesses, let us lay aside every weight, and the sin which doth so easily beset us, and let us run with patience the race that is set before us" (Hebrews 12:1). We read about the many examples of Christian faithfulness in Hebrews 11: "By faith Noah, being warned of God of the things not seen as yet, moved with fear, prepared an ark to the saving of his house; by which he condemned the world, and became heir of the righteousness which is by faith" (v. 7).

We must believe that with God's help we can and will do better. When sinful thoughts come into our minds, we choose to either let them sit there, germinate, or act upon them. We cannot stop thoughts from coming into our minds, but we can determine if we will act upon them or not.

Poor Me Syndrome

We cannot wear the bandages of frustration, tiredness, laziness, and guilt. We have to have repentant hearts daily. We know when we have sinned. Once we sin we are cut off from God. To get back with God, we must repent (turn from sin and toward God) of our sins. Repentance is godly sorrow (2 Corinthians 7:10); not the shame of being found out but the reality of knowing that we have sinned against God. We see David's example of repentance in Psalm 51:3, 4: "For I acknowledge my transgressions: and my sin is ever before me. Against thee, thee only, have I sinned, and done this evil in thy sight: that thou mightest be justified when thou speakest, and be clear when thou judgest." David was sad because he tarnished his relationship with God. He did not think about what man had to say. We often repent when we have been exposed in our sin by others, rather than realizing that God sees and hears all things. Luke 13:3: "[E]xcept ye repent, ye shall all likewise perish." God requires all of us to repent (Acts 17:30). The blessing of repentance is the ability to start over. Repentance helps us not to become habitual and continual sinners. We learn to realize that we answer to a higher calling.

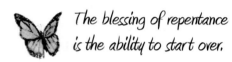

The blessing of repentance is the ability to start over.

I am constantly asking God to save me, save me from myself and from my desires that are not in accordance to His will. I realize without God I am nothing, and I can do nothing! "I can do all things through Christ which strengtheneth me" (Philippians 4:13).

"I am the vine, ye are the branches: He that abideth in me, and I in him, the same bringeth forth much fruit: for without me ye can do nothing" (John 15:5).

Open Your Bible, Grab a Pen and Paper.

1. Explain how you are experiencing God's goodness.
2. What does Psalm 27:1, 4 mean to you?
3. Should you be afraid as you serve God? Why or why not?
4. Give the steps and Scriptures for God's plan of salvation.
5. What does it mean to repent?
6. Name some of the dangerous effects of sin.
7. Name three ways Satan tempts us.
8. How can you develop or maintain a sincere heart?

 Application

In what areas (based upon the three ways we are tempted)
do you find yourself being tempted?

Memorize God's plan of salvation.

Chapter 12
Getting to Know All About God

By reading Luke 10:38–40, I am reminded of the sisters, Mary and Martha, and how Martha willingly allowed Jesus to stay at her home. Mary sat at Jesus' feet and listened to Him teach, while Martha took care of the household chores. Martha got upset that Mary was not helping her with the chores, and she asked Jesus to encourage her sister to help. Jesus said to her, "Martha, Martha, thou art careful and troubled about many things: But one thing is needful: and Mary hath chosen the good part, which shall not be taken away from her" (vv. 41, 42). Mary concluded that time with Jesus was more important than household chores. I'm not advocating keeping a dirty home, but I am suggesting we make wise choices in the use of our time. We need to plan time to spend in study, prayer, and meditation toward knowing God. How wonderful it will be to sit in heaven and fellowship with our Ceator.

Handling Friendship

I think of all the close friends that I have and how we make the most of our time together. Our time may be spent having lunch, discussing a ladies' project, or sharing our joys and sorrows. I always walk away feeling spiritually refreshed and energized. Godly friendships are wonderful and can help us on our

Godly friendships are wonderful and can help us on our Christian journey.

Christian journey. However, a friendship with God is priceless! Consider the example of Naomi and Ruth recorded in Ruth 1:16: "And Ruth said, Intreat me not to leave thee, or to return from following after thee: for whither thou goest, I will go; and where thou lodgest, I will lodge: thy people shall be my people, and thy God my God." What a wonderful relationship between a mother and daughter-in-law. I'm also reminded of the unselfish friendship of Jonathan and David. Jonathan chose to assist his friend in finding safety and go against his own father, King Saul (1 Samuel 18:1; 19:1-7; 20:1-42).

God wants a friendship with us. He wants us to have lunch with Him—and dinner. He wants us to get together for no reason. He wants us to ask Him for advice and seek counsel when we are weary. He wants us to sing songs of praise to Him. He wants us to ask in prayer for wisdom and strength to move forward. He wants us to take Him with us while we jog. God wants us to talk to others about how thankful we are to have Him. He wants us to drop everything and serve Him daily. He is a jealous God (Exodus 20:5).

We may think this type of friendship is too intense. I often look at the big picture; my Creator wanting me to be His friend. The rewards I get from loving Him are far better than anything offered to me in this life. A trophy for doing a good job will *We must long to have a friendship with God.* eventually rust. A diamond ring for being a good wife will suddenly seem insignificant. When we begin to view earthly rewards as temporary, we understand that having our names written in heaven is far more valuable (Luke 10:20).

Desiring a Friendship With God

Desire: to delight in or long for. We must long to have a friendship with God. This has to be established first before we can accept and reap the blessings of this friendship. As we grow toward a sincere friendship with God, our life takes on new meaning. How do we develop a friendship with God?

As I mentioned in the previous chapter we have to obey God's plan of salvation, so we can have the right relationship with God. This relationship must be based upon an individual desire to be saved (Romans 10:1-3). Our zeal (ardent and active interest) must be according to knowledge. This submission must be based upon God's righteousness and not our own way of worshiping Him. The next step is the desire to know and follow God. This comes from our faith, a belief that we know He exists, He created all things, and without Him we can do nothing. "[F]aith cometh by hearing, and hearing by the word of God" (Romans 10:17). We must realize that the more we hear His Word, the more our faith grows. God gave us the breath of life, and the information we receive from His Word is for us. God's Word will help us to become what He created us to be. I have often heard some Christians say, "I have grown up in the church, but I don't really feel that I know God. I question if I have my own individual faith or my parents' faith?" These are great questions to consider.

Do we wear spiritual clothing or the clothing we have created ourselves (Ephesians 6:14-17)? Are you an elder's or deacon's wife? Are you a preacher's wife or the child of a preacher? Are you a stay-at-home mother or a working mother? Are you a single Christian? To find the answer we have to go inward and ask if we have adopted only characteristics from these titles. Do you attend ladies' events because you are an elder or preacher's wife? Or do you attend so that you can grow and encourage someone? Do you stay at home with your children so you can belittle working mothers and make yourself feel superior? Are you depressed about your singleness and attend single functions only to find a soul mate? If we have adopted these "eye view" traits, then we only seek to please ourselves and men. This is doing half the job and expecting full pay. We owe it to ourselves to delve into God's Word. We should partake of the ministries within our congregations to grow more spiritually. The detriment of this thought process can lead us only to be concerned with filling the duties of the title.

If we have been blessed with true friends who tell us the truth in *agape* love, we should thank God for them. Thank God when His Word pricks at our hearts, and we are moved to make changes. Be prepared to make the time to establish and build upon a relationship with God. A friendship with God is a continual feast.

 Thank God when His Word pricks at our hearts, and we are moved to make changes.

Accepting His Word

We must accept His Word as the Word of God. "Sanctify them through thy truth: thy word is truth" (John 17:17). "In the beginning was the Word, and the Word was with God, and the Word was God" (John 1:1).

"Heaven and earth shall pass away, but my words shall not pass away" (Matthew 24:35). "Knowing this first, that no prophecy of the scripture is of any private interpretation" (2 Peter 1:20).

We always ask before beginning a personal Bible study with someone, "Do you believe the Bible to be the Word of God? This question is the foundation of all that we share from that moment forward. If a person does not believe the Bible to be God's Word, why would he or she see the importance of being friends with God?

We can look at nature and see the beautiful mosaic of God's handiwork. I became more appreciative of God's power and wisdom during my pregnancy. The amazement of how God creates life in the womb (Psalm 139:14) and allows, through His providential care, the mother to carry a child for nine months, never ceases to amaze me. I stand in awe of the power of God!

God requires a continual learning and growing from each us. "Study to shew thyself approved unto God, a workman that needeth

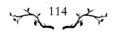

not to be ashamed, rightly dividing the word of truth" (2 Timothy 2:15). "But now, O LORD, thou art our father; we are the clay, and thou our potter; and we all are the work of thy hand" (Isaiah 64:8).

There are different stages of the Christian journey. When we first obey, we are babes in Christ. We drink milk as newborn babies. As we grow (through study) we are able to digest meat as a toddler receives his first drumstick. "[W]hen thou art converted, strengthen the brethren" (Luke 22:32). We have a job to do, and that is why it is vital that we grow spiritually. My son and I sing the song, "Read your Bible and pray every day and grow, grow, grow. Forget your Bible and forget to pray and shrink, shrink, shrink." We attend worship not just to sit on the pews. Prior to leaving home we should have a family or person in mind that we want to encourage. The Bible gives direction and offers guidance to the saved and lost. We have the assurance that God is steering us home.

Abide: **To dwell, to encamp, sit down, to remain.** When we purchase new homes or lease apartments, we take all of our belongings with us. We notify the post office of our new addresses. We may send out moving cards to friends and family so they know where to find us.

In John 15:1–17, Jesus instructs us to abide in Him. He begins by saying that He is the true vine, and His Father is the husbandman (gardener). Every branch that does not bear fruit is taken away. However, the branch that bears fruit is purged to make more fruit. For us to bear fruit we must continually abide in Christ. We cannot bear fruit if we are not abiding. If we are not bearing fruit we are cut down and thrown into the fire. If we are abiding, whatever we ask will be given to us. We will ask in prayer for those things that are godly because we are abiding. As we abide, we experience God's love and joy through obedience. "Ye are my friends, if ye do whatsoever I command you" (v. 14). What a privilege to be called a friend of Jesus. We must abide to experience peace and joy along this journey. "All scripture is given by inspiration of God, and is profitable for doctrine, for reproof, for correction, for instruction in righteousness" (2 Timothy 3:16).

The Real Enemy

"And the Lord said, Simon, Simon, behold Satan hath desired to have you, that he may sift you as wheat" (Luke 22:31). Satan wants us to spend eternity with him in hell! "Be sober, be vigilant; because your adversary the devil, as a roaring lion, walketh about, seeking whom he may devour [to eat, consume]" (1 Peter 5:8). "But the children of the kingdom shall be cast out into outer darkness: there shall be weeping and gnashing of teeth" (Matthew 8:12). Satan is the god of this world. We can see how true this is by how the media encourages immodesty, promiscuity, adultery, and murder.

God has already sealed Satan's fate; and just like the alcoholic, Satan prefers not to drink alone. We must realize and accept that we are in a battle between good and evil. "For we wrestle not against flesh and blood, but against principalities, against powers, against the rulers of the darkness of this world, against spiritual wickedness in high places" (Ephesians 6:12). Satan is constantly challenging our allegiance to God. Satan is on his job, and we need to be on ours.

"But I fear, lest by any means, as the serpent [Satan] beguiled Eve through his subtilty, so your minds should be corrupted from the simplicity that is in Christ" (2 Corinthians 11:3). He attacks us in our weaknesses. We see this in Luke 4:1–13 when Jesus has been in the wilderness for 40 days. Satan demanded that Jesus turn stones to bread and offered Him prestige. Jesus replied, "It is written, That man shall not live by bread alone, but by every word of God" (v. 4).

Jesus had the power to do as He wanted, but He did as His Father wanted. Satan does not attack our strong points. He attacks those things that we are hiding from or are afraid to admit to ourselves and God. If we are feeling alone, he attacks us with depression. If we become ill for a long period of time, he attacks us physically and financially. If we are attempting to rear children, he attacks us with mind mutilation and negative words from others. If we are contemplating obeying the gospel, he may put our physical families against us. If we are not in the habit of attending two worship services on Sunday, he brings out-of-town family members for an afternoon visit. If our children become very ill, he places doubts in our minds of God's providential care. He encourages the young Christian girl who is impatient in finding a husband to marry an unfaithful or non-Christian. He enhances sinfulness through the media and ungodly associates. He encourages the family to buy and buy so that they will work continually and make no time to spend with each other. The overwhelmed mother mentally abandons her responsibility because she feels unappreciated. Satan encourages us not to practice forgiveness in our marriages, so we become numb to each other's needs. He places thoughts of embarrassment so we entice our unwed pregnant daughters to have abortions. He encourages us to put more time and energy into our work and pleasing people, so we have no time for spiritual self-evaluation. We must understand that Satan is real and wants us to suffer with him throughout eternity.

> *Satan does not attack our strong points. He attacks those things that we are hiding from or are afraid to admit to ourselves and God.*

We should run toward God and know that He is there to rescue us. May we strive to be as Jesus was in the wilderness and like Joseph when he came out of his garment to flee sin (Genesis 39:6–12). May we be mindful that "[t]he Lord knoweth how to deliver the godly out of temptations, and to reserve the unjust unto the day of judgment to be punished" (2 Peter 2:9).

Too Good to Pass Up

I am reminded of the gifts for birthdays and holidays that are wrapped so beautifully. I love presents, and the thought of finding a "just because" gift from my husband is wonderful. Satan offers the gifts that he knows will keep us struggling yet wanting more. Those satanic gifts are wrapped so pretty, and we are so eager to find out what's on the inside. These gifts are often too good to pass up.

I'm reminded of a time during my single days. I had just come out of a five-year Christian relationship that did not work out. I was very saddened by the outcome but was determined and prayerful to get through it. He was a nice person. He just was not what God wanted for me. I had always been prayerful about a mate (just as my papa told me to be as a little girl), if marriage was what God wanted for me. I was totally enjoying my singleness, and God sent a delightful and faithful Christian brother in my path. We began our relationship as friends. As time passed, I knew he was the answer to my prayers. I prayed to be able to love him, because I knew he was such an enormous blessing in my life. I was certain that he would make a wonderful Christian husband and father. God, in His infinite wisdom, more than answered my prayer. My love for this faithful Christian grew, and our relationship blossomed just as God waters the earth. His feelings were mutual, and he proposed marriage a week before Valentine's Day.

Satan's gifts to me were first a phone call from my non-Christian college sweetheart that I had not spoken to in six years. A few weeks later I received a phone call from my ex-boyfriend. I did not open either gift. At this time I was more certain of my engagement and my destiny to marry this wonderful, godly man. If I opened those gifts out of flattery or what if, I know that my life would not be where it is today. I daily thank God for the blessing He has given me in my husband.

Choosing to deny self is never easy. When we choose the path toward the strait and narrow, we are better in the long run. "Enter ye in at the strait gate: for wide is the gate, and broad is the way, that leadeth to destruction, and many there be which go in thereat: Because strait is the gate, and narrow is the way, which leadeth unto life, and few there be that find it" (Matthew 7:13, 14).

Fighting to Win

Satan enjoys discouraging us in our thoughts: "I'm not good enough." "I don't deserve it." "I don't fit in!" "If only I had ... " "I could do better if ... " Why can't it be me?" "I knew this was going to happen!'

Satan wants our thoughts to become distorted with worry, guilt, anxiety, and fear. When we allow this to happen, we are unable to be of service to anyone. Philippians 4:8 gives specific instruction for what to set our minds on: "Finally, brethren, whatsoever things are true [sincere real], whatsoever things are honest [sincere, earnest], whatsoever things are just [righteous], whatsoever things are pure [genuine, true, simple], whatsoever things are lovely [beautiful], whatsoever things are of good report [beneficial, kind]; if there be any virtue [moral excellence, power], and if there be any praise [homage, thanksgiving], think on these things."

When we are saturating our minds with positive thoughts and people, we don't live as if we are already defeated. We learn to live victoriously (1 Corinthians 15:57)! We must take inventory of what we are allowing Satan to do in our lives, and relinquish his control through repentance and prayer. We must hate Satan! He is the beginning of evil and the direction toward self-destruction. We must learn to walk circumspectly, looking and being aware of our surroundings (Ephesians 5:15). We don't live in fear. "There is no fear in love; but perfect love casteth out fear: because fear hath torment. He that feareth is not made perfect in love" (1 John 4:18).

We don't live as if Satan will win; rather we know that we serve a God that is all-powerful. We must maintain the desire to cover our minds with the Word of God. Remember the old saying, "An ounce of prevention is better than a pound of cure"? Accepting that Satan is out to destroy and defeat us, we must acknowledge that he will use anything or anyone to deter us from our journey. As we learn to view life through God's eyes, we buffet our bodies. "But I keep under my body, and bring it into subjection: lest that by any means, when I have preached to others, I myself should be a castaway" (1 Corinthians 9:27).

Soldiers prepare for battle by doing practice drills. Therefore, they are prepared for attack. The more we say "yes to God and "no" to Satan, the sweeter our Christian walks become. It is then that truly we can say, "[W]hen I am weak, then am I strong" (2 Corinthians 12:10), because we are relying upon God 100 percent.

Open Your Bible, Grab a Pen and Paper.
1. Who is the enemy?
2. How has Satan manifested himself in the media and world today?
3. What are your weaknesses? How do you think Satan will attack you in these areas?
4. What type of gifts has Satan sent to you?
5. How can you defeat Satan?
6. Who is most powerful?
7. How can you stay in the battle to win?

 Application

Memorize Matthew 7:13, 14.

Memorize 1 Corinthians 9:27.

Chapter 13
Peacefulness of Surrendering

"Peace I leave with you, my peace I give unto you: not as the world giveth, give I unto you. Let not your heart be troubled, neither let it be afraid" (John 14:27). The peace that God gives is not carnal but spiritual. The world offers us peace in jobs, homes, friendships, money, and possessions. God's peace is offered in knowing Him. Peace is having a calm spirit while living in turbulent situations. The ability to have peace while on this time side of life is possible through a consistent relationship with our creator.

We have to fill our minds with the Word to not live defeated and purpose-

Peace is having a calm spirit while living in turbulent situations.

less lives. We decide what we will meditate on daily. Christianity is the ability to control our minds through the wisdom of God. Our prayer lives are not of material requests but of requests for help to stay and run the race. Peace is the certainty of God as our security, hope, and final destination. We learn what it means to serve others and reap the rewards of giving spirits. Peace can exist when we experience God transforming our lives into what He would have us to be. There is no attempt to find our purpose, because He reveals our talents through serving others. We strive to make choices that are directly related to pleasing Him.

Searching in Familiar Places

As we become ill, we quickly go to doctors for relief. Doctors provide prescriptions, and we adhere to taking the dosages. The days progress, and we begin to feel better. God has given us the solution for peace; we just have to surrender. We expect to have some long, drawn-out solution for obtaining peace. We are quick to accept the laws of math and physics; but when it comes to God, we question the solution. We wonder why our lives are full of anger, sadness, bitterness, and frustration. We have chosen not to be spiritual minded. "For to be carnally minded is death; but to be spiritually minded is life and peace" (Romans 8:6). We hold onto our old way of doing things and strive not to change. We must daily ask ourselves: What types of reading materials exist in our homes? How much television are we watching? What messags are TV shows and movies giving us? Who are our best friends? How much time are we spending in study, prayer and meditation? Romans 12:2 tells us, "[B]e not conformed to this world: but be ye transformed by the renewing of your mind." Paying the price for worldliness only leads to costly debt. Families are hindered by choices to compromise the truth. Hypocrisy is practiced for the sake of popularity. It is imperative that we make the decision to walk with God daily.

Possession of a Merry Heart

"A merry heart doeth good like a medicine: but a broken spirit drieth the bones" (Proverbs 17:22). To exhibit a merry heart does not mean that we walk around with constant smiles on our faces. A merry heart comes from the assurance of having a meaningful relationship with God. The benefits spread like rain to those that thirst for God.

"Blessed are they which do hunger and thirst after righteousness: for they shall be filled" (Matthew 5:6). We encourage the lost and those who are in the faith with our cheerful countenances. Lives are uplifted and motivated to follow Christ. The crooked is made straight. The lost find their way. The sad are able to express joy.

How do you know if you possess a cheerful countenance? When times of trial and sorrow come, you search for the good. If you are waiting to conceive and your best friend is blessed to do so before you, you can still rejoice with her. We understand that God is not picking on us when things seem to always turn for the worse. We rest in knowing God's providential care and that He is supporting us.

"Keep thy heart with all diligence; for out of it are the issues of life" (Proverbs 4:23). The importance of guarding our hearts (minds) is vital. The opposite of a cheerful countenance is a broken spirit. This type of spirit dries the bones. We can all attest to either having broken spirits or knowing someone that does. You meet with them, and they end up draining out all of your energy. You are not encouraged or motivated by their presence. The faithful Christian has a great deal to be cheerful about: salvation, repentance, prayer, the Holy Spirit, and more.

> You must love the LORD you God with all your heart, with all your soul, and with all your strength. Always remember these commands that I give you today. Be sure to teach them to your children. Talk about these commands when you sit in your house and when you walk on the road. Talk about them when you lie down and when you get up. Write these commands and tie them on your hands and wear them on your foreheads to help you remember my teachings. Write them on the doorposts of your houses and on your gates (Deuteronomy 6:5–9, *ERV*).

When we learn to love God and practice His principles, living the Word and teaching it to our children will become who we are—and not what we do.

The Dangers of Not Surrendering

Satan fools us into believing that when we sin we are only hurting ourselves. There is danger in not obeying the laws of God (1 John

3:4). Our influence is lost (Proverbs 14:34). We become separated from God when we refuse to repent (Isaiah 59:1, 2). We make bad life decisions and blame God for our days of despair. We begin practicing presumptuous (proud, rash, daring) sins. If we stay in this sinful state refusing to repent, our hears become hardened. God will then turn us over to a reprobate (wicked, corrupt) mind (Romans 1:28). This state of mind cannot repent from sin. "[P]eople draweth nigh unto me with their mouth, and honoreth me with their lips; but their heart is far from me" (Matthew 15:8).

Warning Signs

We begin by straddling the fence, trying to have our cake and ice cream. We place degree levels on sin. We look at others rather than ourselves. We notice all the people in our congregation missing services, and we feel justified in our absence. We begin to be puffed up about our unrighteousness. We develop a film of arrogance that is shown through our behaviors. We speak negatively to others regarding the church doctrine and the people. We stop attending outside activities and only come to the worship that is required of us. We refuse to fellowship with our church families and often leave before dismissal. We find ourselves fellowshiping with the gossipers in our congregation. We discuss our dilemmas with ungodly women who encourage our sinful natures. We use repentance as a resource for getting caught rather than realizing we sinned against God. We spend time daydreaming during worship services.

In Genesis 19:12, 13, 15–17, Lot's family was directed to leave the corrupt city of Sodom and not to look back. Lot's wife looked back, and she became a pillar of salt (v. 26). In the New Testament, we are advised that if we put our hand to the plow and look back, we are not fit for the kingdom of God (Luke 9:62). Once we obey the gospel, we need to press forward. As we strive to grow, our old lives become less desirable. We admit the sinful state of our former life, learn from it, and move toward pleasing God.

Behold Now

The Christian walk is not rigid. However, if having the opportunity to spend eternity in heaven is considered rigid, then I'll take it! There are many freedoms in obeying the gospel. What we give up to follow God is far better than choosing "to enjoy the pleasures of sin for a season" (Hebrews 11:25). Every choice and every action has a consequence. If we choose to do good we reap positive benefits; if we choose to do evil, we reap negative benefits. We reap what we sow, whether it is good or bad (Galatians 6:7).

> Ye shall know them by their fruits. Do men gather grapes of thorns, or figs of thistles? Even so every good tree bringeth forth good fruit; but a corrupt tree bringeth forth evil fruit. A good tree cannot bring forth evil fruit, neither can a corrupt tree bring forth good fruit. Every tree that bringeth not forth good fruit is hewn down, and cast into the fire. Wherefore by thy fruits ye shall know them. Not everyone that saith unto me, Lord, Lord, shall enter into the kingdom of heaven; but he that doeth the will of my Father which is in heaven (Matthew 7:16–21).

> Blessed is the man that walketh not in the counsel of the ungodly, nor standeth in the way of sinners, nor sitteth in the seat of the scornful. But his delight is in the law of the LORD; and in his law doth he meditate day and night. And he shall be like a tree planted by the rivers of water, that bringeth forth his fruit in his season; his leaf also shall not wither; and whatsoever he doeth shall prosper (Psalm1:1–3).

Behold, now is the day of salvation. All we have is the gift of time from God, and we don't know when death will come. It behooves us to "be ye also ready" (Matthew 24:44). No one knows when Jesus will return, but we are always warned to be ready. Second Peter 3:10

tells us that Jesus "will come as a thief in the night." A thief will not call and let us know that he is about to rob our homes. He comes when we are in our routines and unaware. "Wherefore, my beloved, as ye have always obeyed, not as in my presence only, but now much more in my absence, work out your own salvation with fear [respect] and trembling" (Philippians 2:12). We can only give answers to God individually of how we have lived our lives. "Knowing therefore the terror of the Lord, we persuade men" (2 Corinthians 5:11).

What God Has Given Us

God has given us everything that pertains to life and to godliness (2 Peter 1:3). We have all that we need, because the Bible is our road map from earth to heaven. If we seek direction, we should look to the Bible. If we want comfort, we should pray. If we feel ourselves slipping, we should ask for help. If we feel fearful, we should rest on the courage of Jesus. If we are choosing to worry, we should tell Satan to get lost!

> We have all that we need, because the Bible is our road map from earth to heaven.

We are free in Christ! Confidence in going to heaven is not filled with emotion but filled with the assurance of knowing the truth and that it makes us free (John 8:32). "Jesus saith unto him, I am the way, the truth, and the life: no man cometh unto the Father, but by me" (John 14:6).

It is my prayer and heart's desire that this book has uplifted and encouraged you to surrender to God for peace and to keep traveling toward transformation in your life. I pray that you will stay in the race. Keep striving and giving God your heart. I'll keep praying that you trust in the Lord with all your heat; and lean not unto your own understanding. In all your ways acknowledge Him, and God shall direct your paths (Proverbs 3:5, 6).

Shape My Heart

There are voices crying in my head
Telling me which way to go
This way, that way,
Up or down, I feel I'll never know.
I struggle with the roads to take
And with what path to choose
I try to find my own way out
And end up lost and confused.
I'm tired of the struggle.
I'm sick of the strain.
I'm ready to give my life up
To the one who will obtain
I throw off my agendas
And all my "have to" thoughts
My dreams are now as yours are
God, I'll let you shape my heart.

by Tammy Belcher
(rewritten with her permission)

Open Your Bible, Grab a Pen and Paper.

1. How can you receive peace from God?
2. Have you surrendered your heart (mind) to God?
3. How can you learn to be peaceable during adversity?
4. Explain Romans 12:2.
5. What does it mean to have a merry heart?
6. Do you possess a merry heart?
7. Proverbs 4:23 tells us to guard our hearts (minds). How can we do this?
8. What dangers do we face by not surrendering to God?

 **Application**

Memorize Deuteronomy 6:5-9.

How can the poem "Shape My Heart" help you?

CPSIA information can be obtained
at www.ICGtesting.com
Printed in the USA
LVOW10s0549260318
571032LV00004B/6/P

9 780890 985496